Cannonballs & Cranberries

by Fredrika A. Burrows

William S. Sullwold, Publishing
Taunton, Massachusetts

FIRST EDITION

LCCCN 76–3143
ISBN–0–88492–011–9, Hard Cover
ISBN–0–88492–012–7, Paper Cover

TABLE OF CONTENTS

Introduction

n America no Thanksgiving dinner is complete without cranberry sauce. The nostalgic appeal of its bright red color and zestful tartness brings to mind crisp autumn days, joyous homecomings and holiday feasts. Along with the turkey, squash, cornbread and pumpkin pie, cranberry sauce has become the symbol of an American culinary tradition that has lasted over 350 years.

Cranberries, once growing wild on Cape Cod marshes, have become a multi-million dollar industry. A strictly New England delicacy until fairly recent times, this fruit in various forms, — fresh berries, sauce, relish, juice and juice blends — has gained favor in such un-New England places as Texas, Nevada, Oklahoma, and Tennessee, providing a healthful and tasty food for millions of Americans not only at Thanksgiving but also throughout the year.

Did you know that the Cape Cod bogs on which cranberries are now grown and harvested were once the source of the iron in the cannonballs used by the Patriots in the Revolutionary War?

Yes, it's true. Many of the colorful and carefully cultivated cranberry bogs in southeastern Massachusetts were once iron bogs. The early settlers dug iron ore in these wetlands: ore to be smelted on home furnaces and fashioned into desperately needed farm implements, carpenter tools and cooking utensils. And, indeed, the iron bogs in the Colony were a source of iron used in the cannon and cannonballs that armed the American forces in the Revolutionary War, and again in the War of 1812.

Every Federalist manufactory was proud to have a hand in gaining independence from British rule, either by furnishing cannon and ammunition, or by equipping American ships with necessary and important hardware.

Swamps and bogs have played an important part in the industrial life of the area since the landing of the Pilgrims on Plymouth Rock. Having provided pasturage and hay for the first settlers, and having furnished the next generation with iron for their manufactories, the marshlands proved to be the ideal location for the cultivation of cranberries.

No other source can claim to be the progenitor of two present day industries; the great American steel industry, and the thriving American cranberry industry.

Rebecca and Abigail Bates at Cedar Point — Scituate
Painting by F. C. Yohn
owned by (property of) Scituate Historical Society

F. C. Yohn (1875-1933) was a noted illustrator. He worked for Harper's, Scribners's, Collier's and illustrated several books. This painting was one of an historical series painted for the Boston Herald about 1930 and went out as a supplement to the Sunday Edition.

This painting is on permanent exhibition in the lighthouse keeper's cottage on Cedar Point.

Scituate's "Army of Two"

he kitchen in the grey-shingled cottage at Lighthouse Point was filled with the fragrance of freshly baked bread and stewing pumpkin. Seventeen-year-old Rebecca Bates stood at the fireplace stirring the pumpkin which was simmering in a black iron kettle.

"I wish we had at least a taste of sugar," she sighed, her brown eyes wistful. "Pumpkin sweetening is bitter on cornmeal mush. Oh, what I could do with a cup of molasses, — but those Redcoats are determined to starve us out."

"If I were only a boy," Abigail cried, "I'd join the militia and fight the British." Younger than her sister by three years, Abigail had no patience with housework and 'doing without'.

She marched up and down the small room pretending to pipe an imaginary fife in imitation of her big brother.

Rebecca laughed and fell into step behind her beating an imaginary drum. "Look out, Redcoats, — here we come." She soon turned back to the fireplace, however, and spoke on a more serious note.

"Time to get busy. We have our jobs, too. Who would trim the wicks and shine the lamps for the lighthouse if we were boys?"

"It isn't fair," Abigail protested, tossing her brown curls, blue eyes flashing. "We make soap and card wool while the men run the blockade. They do all the exciting things."

"We also have supper ready when Father and the boys come back from unloading ammunition and flour at the dock," said Rebecca briskly. "Those two supply boats were really lucky to make Scituate Harbor without being caught by the British patrol. Come now, build up the fire while I put on a kettle of venison."

Abigail made one last turn in her march, swishing her floor-length skirt in a wide arc. Glancing out the window she was startled to see a British war vessel lying a hundred yards off the Point.

7

"Come quickly, Becky," she cried. "That old man o'war, LaHogue, is off here again. Lord-a-mercy, what shall we do? Here come their barges. They'll burn our boats just as they did before."

Rebecca set the kettle of meat on the hearth and ran to the east window. The sun, shining through the morning fog, revealed an enemy war ship, black and threatening, from which boatloads of marines were disembarking. Resplendent in bright red coats, each carried a gleaming bayonet. An alert coxswain, chanting softly, was at the tiller of each whaleboat. The steady, measured strokes of the oarsmen directed the boats towards the mouth of the harbor.

Rebecca stared in disbelief. How could the vessel have sailed in so close to the Point without attracting their attention? Surely they should have heard them when they furled their sails and dropped their bower anchor. What to do? There was no time to run the two miles to the village by the wagon path to warn the men; the long boats were already approaching the channel entrance.

"It is the British," she gasped. "They've found out our vessels have slipped past their blockade. Our men aren't armed and they'll capture all that ammunition and flour and sugar."

Daughter of a lighthouse keeper, Rebecca was well aware of the purpose of the enemy invaders. The United States had been at war with Great Britain since June, 1812, when she had protested the seizing of American men and ships on the high seas. Since that time Great Britain had maintained a veritable blockade of the settlements along the American east coast. Twice before, that summer, they had entered Scituate Harbor and burned boats loaded with muskets, gun powder, and food which had evaded their patrol.

"What shall we do, Becky?" Abigail's voice trembled and tears filled her eyes. "Could we shoot them with Father's musket as they pass through the entrance?"

"No," replied Rebecca, "we could only fire one volley and stop one boatload. But I have an idea; you take the fife and I'll take the drum. We'll go out behind the dunes where the soldiers can't see us and play Yankee Doodle as loud as our brothers could."

"What good will that do?" asked Abigail.

"Scare them. All you've got to do is scream the fife as Will has taught you and I'll call the roll. They'll think the militia is coming. It will also warn the men of the danger."

Rebecca grabbed the drum, and Abigail, crying softly, followed with the fife. Bending low to hide from the enemy the girls ran out the back door to a level spot behind the yellow dunes.

"Start playing, Abby, and follow me." Striding ahead, almost hidden by the big drum hanging by a thick red cord about her neck, Rebecca pounded the roll with all her might. Abby raised the fife and started to march behind her sister. The instrument felt awkward and damp in her hands and she found the notes with trembling fingers and quivering lips. Back and forth they marched, back and forth, a distance of twenty-five or thirty feet, pounding and blowing as though their lives depended upon it.

The martial sound rose, shrill and strong, high above the roar of the waves pounding on the shore and the screaming of the airborne gulls. Rebecca felt the cord cutting into the back of her neck, the drum bumped her knees with every step. She could hear Abigail gasp for breath, but they must not stop. If they failed the settlement was lost.

The sound of a sharp volley burst over the water. It echoed and re-echoed, drowning out the piping of fife and rolling of drum. Rebecca peeped over the top of a sand dune. The longboats were withdrawing in confusion. The LaHogue, alert to danger, had signalled her men to return.

Rebecca was jubilant. Her plan had succeeded. The British were retreating. "Come on, Abby," she cried, and started to run down the dusty road to the village.

The girls were met by the astonished townspeople who thought the militia from neighboring Cohasset had routed the enemy. Keeper Bates embraced his daughters.

"Good work, girls," he cried. "I am proud of you."

"Becky thought of the fife and drum," said Abigail.

Rebecca laughed, "I couldn't let those Redcoats seize all those provisions, especially after our boats had successfully run the blockade. I do so hope there was sugar in the load, Father. I'm so tired of pumpkin sweetening."

"There's sugar, Becky," said Keeper Bates, "and you've earned your share for this fine performance today."

He turned and gazed out over the harbor. "I doubt that the Redcoats were worrying about a few provisions, however. Our militia has been very active lately. I believe the LaHogue is looking for the foundry at Carver. Our cannonballs are beginning to take their toll."

The enemy had withdrawn, but their interest, as Keeper Bates suspected, had not been in contraband. They were trying to locate a foundry, reported by Loyalists to be in the area.

Since the discovery of iron ore in the Colony, numerous forges and foundries had sprung up and were supplying American patriots with ammunition. These iron manufactories had become a source of irritation to the British. They were determined to seek them out and destroy them.

History of Iron

et us consider, for a moment, the importance of iron. Iron is found almost universally throughout the world, while the use of iron, in its various forms, marks the development of the human race from barbarism to civilization.

It is more needed by man than any other commercial element in the world. Indeed, if we were to be deprived of all gold and silver, we would feel their loss only temporarily. Substitutes would soon be found to take their place. If the world were deprived of iron, all material progress would halt, civilization would regress, and we would become, once again, a primitive people, dependent on the soil and the work of our hands to survive.

The Iron Age was the stage of civilization when men began to use tools and weapons made of iron. It was the last of three prehistoric ages of progress, and followed the Stone Age and the Bronze Age. It began at different times in different parts of the world. Research reveals that the Egyptians were familiar with iron before the time of Moses; that steel was manufactured in India, and its secret very early found its way to Persia and the West under the name of Parthian iron. The Chinese put a tax on it as early as 700 B. C.

In Europe the knowledge of the use of iron developed slowly, beginning in the south and progressing northward, hampered by the lack of communication and early means of travel. Greece was changing from the use of bronze to iron during Homer's time, while Scandinavian countries did not enter their Iron Age until about the beginning of the Christian era. Indeed, for some isolated, primitive peoples the Iron Age has not yet begun.

Implements and weapons were not cast, they were hammered into shape, much as the early settlers in America shaped and hammered their tools. The degree to which the article was perfected was dependent upon the dexterity and skill of the craftsman. It was during the early centuries of this Age that written characters were introduced and a semblance of historic records brought into use.

Iron, in its pure state, is a silver-grey metal with a brilliant luster. It is seven and three-fourths times heavier than water, is highly ductile and malleable, and can be tempered to varying degrees of hardness.

The iron which is dug from the earth is not chemically pure; it contains other materials, such as arsenic, carbon, lime, phosphorus and sulphur. In mines it is often mixed with aluminum, copper, manganese, nickel, and other metals. These foreign substances must be removed before the iron can be made commercially useful. Great smelting works and iron and steel mills have been established throughout the world for this purpose. Steel is included in this category because it is a product of iron that has undergone certain hardening and refining processes.

Common iron ore is rusty-red in color and has the appearance of fine sand that has been burned. That the material has been burned is actually true, for, in the earth, where it has lain for thousands of years, it has been subjected to oxidation which has reduced it to this condition. This type of iron is called "hematite", also known as specular ore, red hematite and fossil ore. The word "hematite" is Greek and means "blood-like"; the name was given to this type of ore because of its reddish-brown color.

Hematite is 70 per cent pure iron and is found in almost all rock formation, even in loose earth. There are other kinds of iron ore such as magnetite, or magnetic oxide which contains 72.4 per cent; brown ore or brown hematite with 60 per cent; siderite, also called carbonate ore and kidney ore, 25 per cent; on down to 20 per cent in what is called 'black band', a form of clay iron-stone. This explains why ore, taken from the ground, must be purified and refined to be of commercial use. Any impurities would have a disastrous effect on the finished product.

The United States contains more iron than any other country in the world. About 93 per cent of this country's ore is hematite, and the greater part of that is now mined in the Lake Superior region of Minnesota and Michigan. The discovery of these deposits and the subsequent industries came as the white men advanced in the opening up of the West in the middle 1800's. This, of course, meant the establishment of huge foundries, steel mills and manufacturing plants in that area, and put an end to the small foundries and mills in the East.

Discovery of
Iron Ore
In New England

he few iron cooking pots and farm tools which the Pilgrims brought with them on the Mayflower were so prized that they were bequeathed in wills along with dwellings, furniture, books and cattle. Most of their implements were made of wood. Indeed, when Governor Bradford and Captain Myles Standish proposed building a Cape Cod Canal, there was not an iron shovel in the country. Ebenezer Tomson, a grandson of Francis Cooke of the Mayflower, had a wooden shovel with a pointed iron end. It was considered so superior to their own wooden spades that it was greatly in demand by his borrowing neighbors.

We can well imagine the Colonists' delight when they discovered iron ore lying in the marshes and streams in their new homeland. It opened up a whole new dimension to their lives, changing hardship to a semblance of comfortable living.

The iron ore discovered by the early settlers in New England was of the brown hematite variety. It lay, loose and porous, in bogs and on the bottom of ponds and streams, or layered in marshes and low-lying meadows. The Pilgrim fathers called it "bog-iron".

You may wonder how iron ore, which we visualize as hard and deeply embedded in underground mines, could be lying in ponds and bogs, easily seen and readily available. The scientific explanation of the iron ore deposits in these areas is interesting and accounts for the industries which resulted from its discovery in New England.

Gneiss rock, which is granite-like rock formed in layers, is impregnated with sulphuret of iron. It is continually undergoing decomposition by the action of air, heat and moisture. It is changed, first into an oxide, then some of it into a sulphate. The oxide absorbs carbonic acid from the atmosphere and is changed into a carbonate which is soluble in water; or the oxide, washed from the rocks into cavities by rain, meets with water containing carbonic acid which dissolves it. Once dissolved, it is easily transported to ponds and swamps where it is deposited, layer upon layer, and becomes bog ore.

Ponds and swamps on the New England seaboard, particularly in Plymouth and Bristol Counties of Massachusetts, had large quantities of oxide and sesquioxide deposited in them. Barbara Chamberlain tells us in "These Fragile Outposts" that, by glacial drift, deposits were spread throughout the southeastern New England region and extended from Iron Mile Hill in Rhode Island to Iron Ore Swamp on Martha's Vineyard, and on into Iron Swamp on Nantucket.

Mixed with vegetable mold and water the deposits partially solidified into spongy iron ore, which was the kind found in the Plymouth area, or crystallized into a harder hydrate as found in the Saugus-Lynn area. The ore constantly collected and renewed itself and, if removed, formed new deposits and might again be collectable after a period of from twenty to thirty years. A single source could give from 100 to 600 tons of ore annually, yielding 25 per cent or more of crude iron. These deposits could still be harvested but, of course, are not useful for practical purposes in modern times.

Since iron implements and tools had been in use in England for quite a period of time, the Mother Country was aware of the value of the discovery of iron ore in the fresh water ponds and swamps in the Colony and, as early as 1628, gave special encouragement to its settlers to search for mineral wealth. By 1641, the General Court was offering further incentives in the way of franchises, exemption from taxes and "other privileges" for the discovery of iron ore and the building of manufactories.

Early
Iron Industries
In The Colony

O nce bog iron was discovered, the problem of reducing it to usable iron arose. It meant furnaces, foundries, forges, men who understood the science of iron, and laborers.

To establish and maintain a manufactory three factors were necessary: (1) nearby meadows, swamps and ponds containing iron ore; (2) forests on the surrounding hills (the best charcoal was made from oak, beech, pine, chestnut, and maple, in that order); and (3) sufficient water and water privileges in the area.

In the beginning blast furnaces were used to reduce the ore to a metal which could be fashioned into the necessary tools, farm implements and household utensils. A century later, when lime and coal could be supplied commercially, cupola furnaces took the place of the early smelting furnaces.

Blast furnaces appear to have been of three types: square, cone and pyramid. Undoubtedly, the square was the earliest type. After experimentation, it was found that the cone, or pyramid top, made for a hotter fire. All were built of native stone, eighteen or twenty feet square at the base, and twenty to thirty feet high. In the front or working sidewall was the working arch from which the molten iron was drawn from the hearth and the slag removed. In the back, or one of the other sidewalls, was the blast arch.

In operation, the furnace is kept full of ore, charcoal and flux, which is fed in at the top. A continuous blast of hot air keeps the fire at white heat and melts the descending mixture, at the same time driving the oxygen from the ore while the flux or limestone removes the impurities. The molten iron trickles down and forms a puddle in a crucible on the hearth with the slag floating on top. This slag is extracted through a "cinder notch" near the top of the crucible; the iron is drawn off, at intervals, through an "iron notch" near the bottom. A water wheel operates the bellows by an arm on the wheel axle, making the whole operation a continuous performance until the "blast" is completed.

Furnishing charcoal for an iron manufactory proved to be a profitable business for farmers who owned timberland on the surrounding hills. One cord of wood yielded about 30-35 bushels of charcoal, one bushel weighing about eighteen pounds. To produce a ton of iron required about 135 bushels, or over a ton, of charcoal; this meant four cords of wood. No wonder the conservationists of the time worried about the depletion of the forests.

In coastal areas, clamshells, so abundant along the shore, furnished the lime necessary for the separation of the iron. It took about 450 pounds of shells to 2600 pounds of ore.

One "blast" usually lasted for a month (some ran as long as five or six months), the molten metal trickling down constantly from the furnace into a stone trough. The process was continuous while the furnace was in operation, necessitating round the clock attendance. Thus the workmen worked in shifts and slept in bunkhouses at the plant.

Too expensive to import in any quantity, the manufacture of iron soon became the backbone of industry in the Bay Colony. The first organized industry in America was established in 1643. Young John Winthrop, Jr., son of the governor of the Colony, had studied at Trinity College in Dublin and had become interested in metallurgy and alchemy. With the discovery of iron ore in the Saugus area, he decided to build an iron manufactory.

In need of money to finance his project, Winthrop journeyed to England in 1641 and there formed a "company of undertakers". The "Company of Undertakers for the Iron Works in New England" was comprised of about twenty-five stockholders, businessmen, lawyers, clergymen, merchants and men interested in the development of iron products. John Winthrop, Jr. was appointed the agent.

The stockholders were interested not only in the economic development of the Massachusetts Bay Colony, but also expected to receive a good return on their investment. There was a growing need for iron since the Irish Rebellion had destroyed nearly all the iron works there. In Europe, where the industry had been seriously crippled by the Thirty Years War, a ready market was also anticipated.

Winthrop remained in England for a year and a half, seeking men experienced in iron-making, laborers, and materials to build the manufactory. At the end of that time, with an advance of a thousand pounds, he engaged the Ann Cleave, her captain and crew, to bring the workmen and materials to New England. One group of workers were Scots, collected from English prisons in which they had been incarcerated, having been captured by Cromwell in the English Civil War. Since they had been accustomed to iron work in Scotland, this selection of workers could not have been better.

The community, which was established and run by the iron works company for its workers and their families, was called Hammersmith. Providing housing and a company store where provisions could be bought on credit, this was probably America's first company owned town.

The Saugus furnace was located on the right bank of the Saugus River, in an area where there was an abundant supply of timber nearby, marshes containing bog iron, and a navigable stream which could be dammed to supply the water power. It was constructed against the side of the hill with a wooden footbridge running out to the top of the furnace.

Workers dug the reddish-brown ore from the marshes and low meadows with mattocks, shovels and hoes, loading it onto oxdrawn carts to be carried to the works.

Extensive timber rights were bought up and the felling of the trees and the conversion of wood into charcoal was accomplished by neighboring farmers.

Other workers labored on the rocks at Nahant, quarrying the black igneous rock which provided the flux. This was a fortunate discovery, since sea shells had not proven to be sufficiently plentiful for the operation.

When the furnace was in operation its noise, activity, and its flaming chimney dominated the countryside. People came to watch and Indians were fearful of the great smoke-belching structure. Picture, if you will, the procession of leather-aproned workers, carrying baskets of ore, charcoal and flux, marching across the connecting bridge to dump their loads into the roaring chimney, then returning across the bridge for a new load.

A huge water wheel turned below, operating a pair of bellows and forcing a constant stream of air into the furnace. This created the intense heat necessary to reduce the iron to liquid form. A pool of molten iron formed on the bottom of the hearth making heat so intense that the attendants had to cover their faces. Since the impurities were lighter in weight they rose to the surface and were drained off.

The furnace was tapped about every ten hours and the molten iron turned out, red hot, into sand molds and allowed to cool. During this stage no onlookers were permitted near the furnace, as one drop of moisture in the mold could cause an explosion.

The resultant bricks were called "pigs" or "sows". Sometimes the liquid iron was poured directly into molds to fashion pots, skillets, and firebacks, but these products were brittle and their use limited. Iron that could be hammered and made into durable tools was refined in the forge.

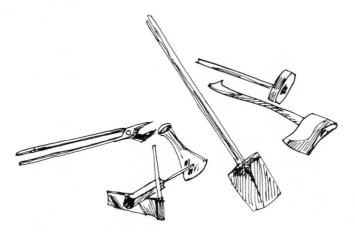

In this process the pigs were reheated, a rock-like "bloom" was formed and drawn across metal plates to be beaten by triphammers and further impurities driven out. The product so treated became wrought or bar iron and from it was fashioned the needed hammers, chains, spikes, nails, anchors, and other tools.

A third building at the works at Saugus was a rolling and slitting mill. One of only about twelve in the world, the machinery in this mill was the most complicated of all the equipment in the Works. Exerting tremendous pressure, it rolled and pressed red-hot iron bars to a desired thickness for "flats". Many flats were used in the construction and repair of the works itself; others were reheated, passed through cutting discs and became rods or bars. Sold by the piece or in bundles, these rods made it more convenient for the farmer-builder to fashion his own nails, tires for wagon wheels, and bands for wooden barrels.

Poor management, high production costs, a fixed price established by the General Court in competition with the price of imported iron, all added up to failure to produce a profit for the stockholders and they refused to advance more capital. There was some apprehension on the part of the local inhabitants that the demand for charcoal for the iron works would be so great that it would deplete the forests in the area to the vanishing point and they did not give wholehearted support to the industry. The decline in production, the departure of skilled workmen to other areas, forced the Saugus Iron Works to reduce production and it finally closed down around 1670.

An intriguing story is told of pirates dropping anchor in the Saugus River and retiring to "Pirates' Glen" where they supposedly hid their treasure. From the top of the craggy rocks they could keep a lookout to observe the travel up and down the river, and the comings and goings of the iron workers.

One day a workman at the foundry found a note near the works stating that if certain tools, including shackles, hatchets, and chains were left in a designated spot, silver would be left there the following night in payment.

Since the villagers were in mortal fear of the pirates, they complied with the request. However, the captain on a King's cruiser, reconnoitering nearby, heard of the plot and had several members of his crew follow the pirates. They captured three of them and executed them before the silver was delivered. A fourth, Thomas Veal, escaped with the plunder and hid in a cave nearby. Before he was able to leave, however, he was buried in the great earthquake of 1658.

Nearly two centuries later excavations were made by Hiram Marble on the strength of "revelations I had of pirate treasure" but the search was fruitless. The silver treasure will probably never be found, if indeed it is still there, as the area is "now controlled by the Public Forest Trustees", according to Katharine Abbott's "Old Paths and Legends of New England".

In 1644 Winthrop's company moved to "Brantry" and set up a second plant on the Monautiquet River, with Thomas Leader as General Agent. The first commercial iron was produced here and was the forerunner of this country's great iron and steel industry.

A distinguished metallurgist, a Dr. Child, who had worked with the company at Saugus, joined them at Braintree, and, under his direction, tons of cast iron hollow-ware (kettles, pots, skillets, "stoves") were produced and shipped throughout the country. Dr. Child did not stay with the company long. He had joined with Mr. Daud, Mr. Maverick and Mr. Vassall in petitioning Governor Winthrop for religious tolerance, particularly for Episcopalians, been refused and fined. Angered and discouraged, he gave up manufacturing of iron and any plans he had for a glass-works and a black lead mill.

At that time, the town of Braintree encompassed a large area (it is now divided into the towns of Braintree, Quincy, Holbrook and Randolph). To encourage the ironworks the town granted 3000 acres of common land and "other privileges" to the company. The Court was anxious for such enterprises to succeed and granted as many franchises as possible, land, privileges for forges and refineries, exemption from taxes for the works and the stock for a period of ten years, and a monopoly for making bar iron for under twenty pounds per ton.

The workmen were freed from military training and were permitted to invest up to twenty pounds in the stock of the corporation. By 1645 the manufactory had become so successful that the twenty pound limit was raised to one hundred pounds. It is interesting to note that salaries were paid in various commodities besides money, some of these being beaver skins, wheat, corn and oil. The workmen were also permitted to take any timber, stones, iron ore, clay or furze that they wanted and were given the right to build projects, such as roads, dams, and waterways for their own use in any unclaimed waste places.

Plymouth Colony
And North River
Area

here were no communal industries or cooperative businesses carried on in the Plymouth Colony. After a brief trial period of community-owned gardens and collective preparation of the food and washings by the women-folk, it was decided that it was unfair for a man's wife to do such household work for other men, and the Colony returned to the former way of each household attending to their own needs.

For almost fifteen years thereafter, the Pilgrims, finding themselves in an alien and hostile country, were concerned with their own preservation: protection from the Indians, maintenance of their rude dwellings against the vagaries of the New England weather, hunting and fishing, clearing land on which to plant crops of corn and beans, and gathering berries and nuts and storing them against hunger that threatened during the long winter months.

Once they were established, however, and had become reasonably friendly with the neighboring Indians, they began to realize the advantages of trading with the Indians and with the other coastal colonies. They began to build vessels and to set up packet lines along the New England seaboard.

In the early days many of the vessels built were engaged in the coasting trade; the different colonies set up trading posts, trading both with the Indians and with vessels that came for that purpose.

Winthrop wrote in 1634: "Our neighbors of Plymouth had oft traded with the Dutch at Hudson's River, called by them 'New Netherlands' ".

In his Journal of September 1632, Governor John Winthrop told of exploring the territory northwest of Plymouth, now encompassing the towns of Hanover and Pembroke.

"About five in the morning the Governor (Winthrop) and his company came out of Plimouth. The government of Plimouth (Bradford) with the Pastor and Elder & c, bringing them nearly one-half mile out of town in the dark. Lieut. Holmes with two others and the Governor's mare came along with them to the great river, (now called North River), they were carried over by one Luddam, their guide, — the stream being very strong and up to their crotch, so the Governor called the passage Luddam's Ford".

The North River proved to be of the utmost importance to the Colonists. To the early settlers it provided large supplies of food, as it and its tributaries abounded in many kinds of fish; herring or ale-wives, shad, smelts, bass, pickerel, white and red perch, horn-pout, and a certain variety of salmon.

For most people the fame of the North River was spread through its shipbuilding industry and the many famous ships which were launched from its banks. Several historical events also took place along the banks of this noted river, many of which included the iron ore with which we are presently concerned.

In searching the Plymouth records for early iron works we find: "In 1648, Mr. Timothy Hatherly, the principal founder and father of the town of Scituate, requested liberty of the colony to erect an iron mill. It was granted in 1650, on condition that it be erected within three years, or the privilege and certain woodlands about the Mattakeeset Pond (now Pembroke) were to revert to the Colony. It did not take place, however, during that period, but a smelting fur-nace was erected on the precise grant by Mark Despard and the Barker family about 1702.

With the discovery of the North River (the boundary line between Scituate and Marshfield) and its tributaries, the Indian Head and the Namassakeesett River, others recognized its possibilities and set up manufacturing plants.

The North River area was particularly conducive to the iron in-dustry for several reasons, two of the most important being: (1) the numerous ponds and bogs in the immediate vicinity abounded in "bog-iron" ore which was easily available; and (2) plenty of water power to turn the wheels of the mills.

In 1704, Thomas Bardwin built a dam just above Luddam's Ford and erected a forge nearby. He supplied the increasing demand for anchors and knees for the vessels being built downstream. The business prospered and was inherited by his son who was successful and important enough to merit, at his death, the following notice in the Boston Evening Post, dated Feb. 14, 1774: "Died — At Hanover, Capt. Thomas Bardwin, aged 86. He was born near Haverford — West, in South Wales, came over in 1716, and was the first that made bar iron in New England".

The "old iron works" in Hanover, consisting of a forge and iron foundry, was built and operated by Joseph and Thomas Josselyn. In 1740 they were succeeded by Seth, Philip, Isaac and John R. Josselyn, Lemuel Dwelley, Benjamin Studley and Lemuel Curtis. The business was a thriving one, turning out anchors and doing the iron work for vessels being built down river during the late 1700's and early 1800's. By buying out other members of the company and through inheritance, Mr. George Curtis became the sole owner in 1831. Several anchors for the grand old warship Constitution were forged here, according to Mr. L. Vernon Briggs in his book "History of Shipbuilding on North River", and during the War of the Rebellion many anchors, some weighing five tons, were made for the United States government. "For over one hundred and fifty years the loud din of the descending hammer could be heard here daily".

In 1720, Colonel Jesse Reed of South Hanover bought out Enos Bates' privilege on Indian Head River and built a dam, locating a grist-mill, nail factory and machine shop nearby. Reed was the inventor of the tack machine, used in the late 1800s with few improvements. His other inventions, twenty in all, include patterns for pumps, cotton gins, and tree-nail machines.

Farther up the river, in 1720, the town granted two acres of land to Captain Joseph Barstow and Benjamin Stetson "for the accommodation of a forge and finery". A bridge was built across the river and Barstow's Forge erected. When Joseph died in 1728, his youngest son, Joshua, aged eight, inherited Barstow's interest in the forge. When Joshua was old enough to run the business he took over, made improvements, and ran it successfully until he was drowned in 1763 at the age of forty-four. His son, Joshua, was fourteen years old when he inherited the works and was soon running the forge capably and profitably. During the Revolution he carried on quite a business in the manufacture of cannon balls, melting the iron in the ordinary forge and molding the cannonballs in the bottom of the forge.

This Joshua sold the property when he moved to Exeter, New Hampshire in 1795, to Robert Salmond and others who, in 1813, were "making some large anchors for the Frigate that is building at Charlestown".

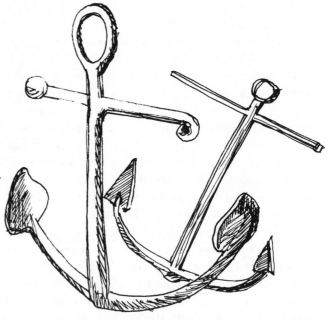

Having worked in the forge for several years Thomas-Hobart became a partner, and in 1825, Hobart and Salmond had a contract with the United States government for the manufacture of anchors for the Navy, several being made for the old 74-gun ships, the largest ever forged.

In 1828 Salmond sold out to Hobart who took John Sylvester into the firm. Sylvester had been a tack-maker and had also been employed at the "Old Mill Dam Iron Works" at Boston and Watertown. About 100 tons of bar iron were turned out here per year, 100 tons of anchors, and twelve to fourteen tack machines were run simultaneously. In 1830 they began the manufacture of locomotive cranks. This partnership was dissolved in 1837 and Sylvester formed the Hanover Forge Company.

The inland area of the North River and its tributaries, with its encompassing iron bogs, forests, river-ways, and the resultant mills made Hanover one of the busiest and most prosperous towns in the Commonwealth. The New England Gazetteer reported in 1839: "Hanover is a manufacturing place, — manufacturing bar iron, iron castings, anchors, plows, vessels, tacks, leather boots and shoes, and woolen cloth, annually to the amount of $75,000.00": a thriving community for those days.

Caleb and Robert Barker had a foundry on the Drinkwater near its joining with the North River. The following advertisement appeared in the Boston Gazette on January 15, 1754:

"Caleb and Robert Barker in Hanover: Cast Bells for Meeting Houses and other uses, from a smaller to a greater, even to one or two thousand weight; cheaper than they can be imported: By whom all persons may be supplied on reasonable terms". A descendant of Caleb and Robert, Joshua Parker, erected an iron foundry, about 1830, on the old site and produced cast hollow-ware, stoves, and "machinery of all types".

Mighill's Works were also situated on the Drinkwater. The son of Reverend Mighill, who was called to Scituate's Second Society in 1684, erected the Works about 1710, getting his ore at "Cricket Hole" near Third Herring Brook and in the Dam Brook area. The story is told that, during the Revolution, cannon were cast here and carted down to the site of the old fulling mill and tested. A workman, Tilson Gould, was killed when a cannon burst while it was being tested, the only death recorded from cannon in the making!

Brooks Mill, originally built by Joseph Brooks in 1820, stood on Longwater Brook where it forms a junction with Drinkwater. Used as a grist mill and then a shingle mill, this site gains historic fame, too, for it was here that the inventor, David Prouty, polished the first cast iron plow ever made.

Other iron manufactories, saw mills, shingle mills, and box factories sprang up, were productive for a time, and then either burned or succumbed to modernization. Their number, their variety and quantity of production, however, attest to the importance of the North River and its contribution to the prosperity of the times.

Iron And Associated Industries In The South Shore And Cape Cod Areas

bout the year 1628 several Pilgrim fathers, feeling that Plymouth was getting crowded and wishing more land on which to farm and graze cattle, moved their families across the bay. They called their settlement "Duxborough" in honor of Myles Standish's ancestral home, Duxborough Hall in Lancashire, England.

It was the first town to buy land from the Indians and to receive a deed from the Indian chief. The area was known as Mattakeeset and was deeded to Myles Standish, Samuel Nash and Constant Southworth by Massasoit on a deed imprinted with his "signature", a human hand with the index finger pointing to the terms of the agreement: "In consideration of the aforesaid bargain and sale, we, the said Myles Standish, Samuel Nash and Constant Southworth do bind ourselves to pay unto the said Ousamequin for, and in consideration of, the said tract of land, as followeth:—

> Seven coats, a yard and a half in a coat
> Nine hatchets
> Eight hoes
> Twenty knives
> Four moose skins
> Ten yards and a half of cotton
>
> > Signed: Myles Standish
> > Samuel Nash
> > Constant Southworth

We note that, in payment, ironware was included in the articles traded for the land. Before the arrival of the Pilgrims the Indians had only wooden and stone tools and implements; metal was highly regarded and eagerly sought in trade with the white men.

The Colonists had a standing order in England for ironware in exchange for goods which they sent to the homeland. Each arriving ship included tools and implements which the Pilgrims needed for their own use and for trading with the Indians.

Plentiful supplies of iron ore were found early in the ponds and swamps in Island Creek, Tarkiln, Tinkertown and North Duxbury and a forge was set up on Hall's Brook (now a part of Kingston). The ore was carted down a road called, appropriately, Old Forge Road. It appears that the tools and hollow-ware produced locally, were for the needs of Duxbury families and no commerical industry established although castings were made for the many shipyards on Blue Fish River, Eagle's Nest Creek and Island Creek.

A deed was given in 1728 which read: "Know all (men) by these presents, that, I, Joseph Holmes, of Kingston, in the County of Plymouth in New England, in consideration of twenty-five pounds to me in hand, paid me by Ephraim Holmes of Kingston aforesd, do give, grant, bargain and sell on sixteenth part of a forge or iron mill built by Benjamin Eaton, William Cook, Benjamin Sampson, Thomas Cook, Ephraim Holmes and myself on land of Ephraim Holmes aforesd, on a certain stream called and known as Hall's Brook, with all my rights and privileges in the sd forge, and the right to carry and recarry Coal and Iron Mine (ore) as I had it of Ephraim Holmes".

The making of iron created many other industries and brought prosperity to bordering neighborhoods. The making of charcoal was a thriving adjunct. Remnants of charcoal and charcoal pits are still found where tons of charcoal were made in burners in North Duxbury. They not only supplied the local forge but sent it also in carts over the sandy roads to Pembroke and Taunton.

In the making of charcoal wood was stacked in a vertical position forming a solid dome-shaped pile which would be set on fire, covered with earth and sod, and left to smolder, the slower the burning the better the charcoal. Smoke from the numerous pits would hang in the air for miles around.

For years new locations containing iron ore continued to be found, while areas which had been harvested continued to be renewed. This made it possible for ponds to be redredged and bogs to be redug after a period of about twenty-five to thirty-five years.

Sometimes the discovery of new deposits was entirely by accident. In 1751, a century after the building of the first works, Joseph

Holmes was fishing in Jones River Pond in Kingston. He caught a piece of ore on his hook. The yield from this source was so high that it produced 3000 tons of 25 per cent iron before it was allowed to settle and begin the renewal process. Metal from this deposit became known as "Holmes iron", much of it being cast into cannon balls for Washington's army.

A deposit was found in Assawompset Pond in Middleborough in 1760 which yielded 600 tons a year for a long period of time and was still producing at a profit in 1820.

Ownership and disposition of the iron ore in the bogs and ponds of the various towns proved to be a problem. After the discovery of iron ore and the resulting establishment of forges and foundries there was a mad scramble by those living near ore-yielding waterways and marshes to begin to harvest it and sell it to the manufactories. The several townships claimed ownership of ore lying within their boundaries, and hired labor to excavate it and cart it to the foundries, the proceeds to go into the town treasury.

According to the Plympton Parish Town Records, iron ore in the Jones River Pond was discussed at the May 21, 1773 meeting and "Mr. Ephraim Bryant was chosen to take care of the Iron Ore in Jones River Pond and make the best of it for the Town". As late as 1808 an agent was chosen "To take care of the iron ore in Jones River Pond".

In the same record books on May 9, 1748 at a "Town meeting held at the Old Meetinghouse in Plimton" Mr. George Samson and Mr. Benjamin Weston were the committee appointed "respecting the Iron Ore in Samson's Pond" and were given instructions "to search in the Proprietors' Records of Plymouth and also the Records of the ( ) Deeds to see whether said Pond is included in either of them and also to examine in any other Records as they shall think fit and make return of their doings at the next Town meeting".

"At a Town meeting held at the South meeting house in Plimton, July 4, 1748" the Committee reported that "said Ore belonged to the Town". Their report was accepted and then the Town proceeded to choose "the former Committee to procede further with respect to said Ore and to act according to such instructions as said Town shall think fit".

It was also voted "that the Committee aforesaid shall forthwith employ 2 or 3 men to dig Ore in said Pond and if they are molested, to sue any that shall presume to dig Ore in said Pond without order from said Committee and also to seize any Iron Ore they can prove was taken out of said Pond".

On May 15, 1749 at Old Meeting House in "Plimton" the members of the Town "Voted further to inploy the Committee that was chose relating to the Iron Ore at Samson's Pond to appear at the next Superior Court to be holden at Plymouth in behalf of said Town".

They were successful in their suit and at a meeting held September 11, 1749: "Mr. Samuel Wright was chose to act in said Town's behalf respecting the Iron Ore in Samson's Pond and gave him instructions as followeth: to order the digging and carting said Ore for the use of said Town and to prosecute any persons that shall presume to act on anything respecting said Ore without his order and to settle accounts with those that have already carted ore from said Pond or otherwise to prosecute them in the law and to make his report at March meeting next".

Carver

orty years after the landing of the Pilgrims at Plymouth Rock, settlers moved out to South Meadows — then a part of Plympton. When the town was separated, in 1790, this area was included in the town of Carver.

Two of those holding grants were Thomas Pope and George Watson. Pope's land was situated at the junction of Watson's Cove Brook and the Weweantic River, and subsequently became known as Pope's Point. Watson took the land near Rocky Meadows Cove.

A grandson of George Watson, Jonathan Shaw, came into possession of Pope's Point and, in 1735, ceded the water privileges and adjacent land for the first iron manufactory in the town of Plympton (Carver). It was a neighborhood undertaking. The deed to Isaac Lothrop, Esq., Isaac Lothrop, Jr., Lazarus Lebarron, John Cooper, all of Plymouth; to George Barrows, Samuel Lucas, Elisha Lucas, Barnabas Shurtleff, Abel Crocker, Isaac Waterman, Isaac Churchill, John Shaw, and Joseph Lucas, of Plympton, reads: "   for divers good causes but principally and more especially for the encouragement and ye erecting of a furnace or new iron works at a place called Popes Point, in ye town of Plymton, at a place on said land where it shall be most convenient to locate a furnace, coal house or coal houses, pot or pot houses, dwelling house or dwelling houses, or any other building that may be necessary for carrying on said business, also right to a dam already made on Watson Cove Brook and flow land from September 1st to march 31st, two acres of land for a coal yard and mine yard, — the deed to remain in force so long as the men, or the major part of them, keep up the furnace or iron works".

Pope's Point Furnace manufactured hollow-ware, pots kettles, tea kettles, cauldrons, flat irons, bake pans, fire dogs or andirons. It is claimed that the first tea kettle in America was made in this furnace.

The furnace continued in operation until 1835, upwards of a century, a record equaled only by the Charlotte, giving life and prosperity to industrial Plympton.

One of the reasons for the success of the iron industry in Carver was the numerous great ponds in Carver and Halifax which gave over one hundred tons of ore over a long period of time.

The rich bed in Samson's Pond proved to be a bone of contention, the abuttors mining the ore and taking the profit. The Town officials questioned their ownership and took the matter to Town meeting where the decision was in favor of the Town.

The matter did not end there, however. After years of charge and countercharge, the Courts decided in favor of the private claimants, George Barrows and Bartlett Murdock.

In 1760 Murdock began construction of a blast furnace, the following being promotors and partners: James Hovey, William Thomas, both of Plymouth; James Murdock, Nathaniel Atwood, Benjamin Shurtleff, Peleg Barrows, John Bridgham, Frances Sturtevant, Benjamin Barrows, Nathaniel Atwood, Jr., Joseph Barrows, all of Plympton; Robert Sturtevant and Benjamin Curtice, of Halifax.

By 1784 Lieutenant Thomas Drew had bought up "23/32 per cent" of the business, and later that year transferred it to Joshua Eddy of Middleborough. After operating the business for six years Eddy sold it to a partnership of local investors and furnacemen who continued operating it until 1804. By this time it was known as the Charlotte Furnace. In its last years it became a part of Ellis Foundry Company, an operation, in all, of 145 years.

The Charlotte Furnace was said to be named for Princess Charlotte, who later became Queen of England, wife of King George III. At that time Europe was in turmoil, with both France and England struggling for supremacy on the American continent; a contest that ended when England came into possession of Canada through the defeat of General Montcalm by British General Wolfe at Quebec. To show their loyalty, or perhaps to win royal favor, places and buildings were often named for English royalty. Thus, we find a furnace in Carver, Massachusetts, named for an English princess.

One of the best known of the early proprietors of Carver furnaces was Benjamin Ellis. Born in 1774, Benjamin began working in local puddling mills at an early age and became an excellent iron master. A successful business man, he took part in local affairs and gained a reputation for good judgment and for being an astute politician. He became a member of the Massachusetts legislature, and was subsequently called "The Castiron Senator".

In the War of 1812 Ellis obtained a government contract to furnish iron cannon balls for the American Army. To carry out the contract it was necessary to gain control of several furnaces, one of which was known as the Federal Furnace, a name later perpetuated in the Federal Cranberry Company.

The Federal Furnace was located near the source of Crane Brook, having formerly been established in 1793 as a sawmill by General Silvanus Lagell.

The Ellis blast furnaces supplied the shot for the "Constitution", and it is claimed that the British frigate "Java" was so badly smashed by Carver castiron that she could not be salvaged and had to be blown up.

The War of 1812 was conducted under the administration of President James Madison. This was an unpopular war and deeply resented by the Federalists in New England, since it raised havoc with New England shipping. For this reason Mr. Ellis and his business of making cannon balls was not altogether popular either. To prevent sabotage and disruption of his operations he had to put guards around the furnaces at night.

As the demand for ammunition became greater and every available man was needed for the foundry, the women took their turn at standing guard during the day.

Sabotage was not the only problem; with information furnished by Loyalists, the British conducted sneak attacks on known furnaces to try to destroy the sources of the American ammunition supply.

When she was thwarted in her attempt to land at Scituate Harbor, the LaHogue sailed down around the Cape and entered Wareham Narrows, six miles south of Carver, where American farmers, with true aim and quick trigger fingers, prevented them from landing. The Redcoats retreated once again, still unsure of the location of the ammunition plant.

Ellis made a fortune out of his dealings with the government and, at the end of the war, Ellis Company owned its own ships, sailing out of Wareham and Plymouth. The Ellis Company continued making ironware for domestic use and manufactured stoves and hollowware for the foreign trade. Benjamin Ellis died in 1852 leaving a fortune of $200,000.00, a fabulous sum in those days.

Following Ellis' death, his son-in-law, Jesse Murdock, took over the management of B. Ellis & Co. and changed the name to M. Ellis & Co., under which the business continued until it was incorporated as the Ellis Foundry Co.

Murdock conducted a profitable and successful business and at the time of his death was considered one of the wealthiest men and the largest land owners in Plymouth County.

Carver had eight blast furnaces during the period 1735-1835, namely: Popes Point, 1735; Charlotte, 1760; Federal, 1793; Fresh Meadows, 1800; Slug, 1819; South Meadows, 1824; Barrows, 1825; and Wenham, 1827. The first three were in use for many years; the others were short-lived.

We read of an interesting side-light on the furnace at Fresh Meadows. It seems that this furnace was located on a small brook carrying water from New Meadow Swamp to Samson's Pond. There was not enough water power generated to turn the water wheel, even for so small a blast furnace, and so "Cuffy", a black man, became one of the earlist 'motors' to supply air for a furnace. He spent long hours each day swinging a pendulum made of a long pole and a block of wood.

Nail-Making
In Wareham

ron ore was discovered early in Wareham by men who moved their families away from the Plymouth settlement in order to acquire larger farm areas and greater opportunities for fishing. Far from the parent colony, with communication slow and difficult, the settlers had to depend upon their own ingenuity and the resources at hand for their livelihood.

With the discovery that the nearby ponds and marshes abounded in iron ore, the opportunity for making farm implements and needed household utensils opened up with each family meeting its own requirements by making these tools by hand.

Nearly every home had its own furnace and forge. In those early days pots, kettles, forks, spoons, hammers and nails, were pounded into shape during the long winter evenings by the head of the household and the older boys.

Sitting next to the open fire, his work lighted by the leaping flames, the craftsman pounded, shaped and pointed the nails with his hammer on a small anvil (if he were lucky enough to own one) or a stone held on his knees.

In Wareham the making of nails became a handicraft, and as the volume of their product increased beyond their needs, an outside market was set up, and Wareham's nail industry was born.

In 1819, Parker Mills, the first little community cooperative nail-making plant, was set up on the Wankinquoah River. The nail-making machine, which begins with a sheet of iron and turns out a finished nail, was invented by Jesse Reed of Marshfield in 1818. It came into general use when Isaac and Jared Pratt purchased the right to use it, and in 1822 erected a small rolling mill at Bump's Dam, the lower dam on the Wankinquoah. This firm was among the first in the United States to manufacture nails on a large scale.

The business was so successful that, in 1828, they built the Tihonet Works at Tihonet, "Place of Many Cranes". These works consisted of one of the largest and best rolling machines in the country, and included puddling furnaces, and over fifty nail machines. Tihonet derived their power from the Wankinquoah River at the point where it was joined by Robert's Run and Frogfoot, making a twenty-eight foot fall at Tihonet dam.

On a petition by the Pratts, Tihonet, which had originally been a part of Carver and Plymouth, became part of Wareham by an Act of the Legislature in 1827.

At that time a new dam was erected at Bump's Dam raising the water twenty-eight feet and forming a large reservoir. A two hundred rod canal was built from the Tihonet Dam to the head of the lower dam through which scows, carrying plate to be cut into nails, were poled. From there nails were carried through two locks to the docks at Wareham Narrows. The scows were loaded with iron and coal for the trip back up the canal. These undertakings were conducted by Wareham Iron Company until 1834 when they failed and were bought out by John Avery Parker, William Rodman and Charles W. Morgan.

The Tihonet Works, run by Mr. Parker until 1837, were picked up and operated by Nye and Bent, Nye and Lothrop, and Nye and Fearing in succession. Although there was a change in ownership, William Caswell remained superintendent, and it was under his supervision that Parker Mills gained their reputation for excellence and a readily-marketable product in this country and throughout the world.

In 1822 Colonel Bartlett Murdock, formerly superintendent of the Ellis furnaces, and George Howland built the Washington Iron Works on the Weweantit River, in Tremont. This was a large rolling mill and nail factory containing thirty-five machines. A year later they erected a second dam and built a forge for making bar iron out of scrap iron by a rolling process. The property eventually became a part of the Tremont Iron Company.

At one time there was a blast furnace for making pots and kettles, which were fashioned by running iron directly from the smelting furnace into the molds, a rolling mill for rolling and slitting nail plate and for rolling hoops, and a nail and a tack factory. All were eventually incorporated into one ownership, the Tremont Iron Company.

The Tremont Iron Company was organized in 1845; its first president was Nathan Carruth, its directors William Thomas, John Williams, Charles Hayward and James Hayward, all of Boston. They erected puddling furnaces and a rail mill. The rail mill proved to be unprofitable but, by March 1847, it was reported that "about 2100 tons of nails have been made, and, during the past week 100 tons of iron has been puddled". They began the manufacture of nails on a large scale.

In 1858 the Tremont Iron Company sold its entire assets to a new corporation, the Tremont Nail Company. Though burned out in 1860, the plant was rebuilt and in operation by 1867. Its first officers were Richard Soule of Boston, President, and Joshua B. Tobey, of Wareham, Treasurer.

The Tremont Nail Company continues to the present time, a lineal descendant of the early iron works in Wareham. It is a thriving business which enjoys a world-wide reputation for the excellence of its cut nails, for durability, for exceedingly small percentage of impurities, and for rust resistance.

In their Centenary Catalogue, 1819-1919, Tremont Nail Company quotes from "Poor Richard" to prove a point:

"A little neglect may breed mischief —
For want of a nail the shoe was lost
For the want of a shoe the horse was lost
For the want of a horse the rider was lost."

Bridgewater's Contribution To Industry

ew places have done more toward the introduction and promotion of the manufacturing and mechanical arts than the town of Bridgewater. Settled by men and women from nearby Duxbury, the town was incorporated in 1656.

The making of small arms commenced in Bridgewater, many stand of arms being made well before the Revolution. By the beginning of the war cannon, cast solid and bored, anchors, cotton gins, sugar mills, shovels, edged tools, hoops, castings, nails and tacks were being produced.

The prestige and recognition of Bridgewater's industry is due, largely, to Hugh Orr, a mechanical genius and a pivotal figure in the development of industry in America.

Orr was a young Scotsman who settled in Bridgewater in 1740 and began to manufacture edged tools. Ships' carpenters and other workmen in need of cutting tools came from great distances to consult with him and to buy his products. He introduced scythes, axes, a trip hammer, and made the first spinning machine.

In 1748 Hugh made 500 muskets for the Province which were stored in the "Castle" at Boston. Unfortunately, these arms were carried off by the British during the evacuation in 1776.

There was a foundry near Titicut Bridge which cast cannonballs and cannon. The following is an order which they received from the War Office, dated "10th Feb., 1779":

"Sir,— You are required to proceed to Titicut to prepare the metal from the common ore for casting twenty twelve pounders for the ship Protector, which are to be bored completed and finished by the first of May next. You are also to direct the boring of the twenty-four pound cannon that they may be finished without loss of time. Col. Orr will give you every assistance that you may want and should anything further be necessary, the board will finish it.

Wishing you a pleasant journey and are with much regard your friend and very humble servant.   John Brown PPS."

Honorable Hugo Orr (he had become a state senator by the end of the war) heard of two young Scotsmen, Robert and Alexander Barr, who had gained a reputation for unique inventions in their country. Orr invited them to come to this country to construct carding, spinning and roping machines at his plant.

In November 1786, the General Court, recognizing the Barrs' ability and the value of their inventions, by a resolve, allowed them 200 pounds, and later also gave them six tickets to a land lottery (one of the ways in which land was distributed).

Orr kept the machines for display and was requested by the Court to exhibit them, to explain the way they worked, and to give pertinent information to all interested persons.

In the early days guns were handmade and the artisan worked in his home or private shop. He would receive a commission to fashion a rifle or pistol to the buyer's specifications in regard to shape, carving, metalwork and engraving. Each piece was individually made and a work of art. Such guns have become collectors' pieces and bring thousands of dollars.

The demand for guns was so great during the Revolution that individually-made pieces were inadequate to take care of the needs of a country preparing to go into battle, and gun factories sprang up. Orr enlarged his plant. A factory was built in Sutton, and another in Leicester, where a famous gunsmith, Thomas Earle, resided and worked.

In 1778-79 Congress established works in Springfield where cannon were cast and forged (small arms were not made there until after the end of the war). The present National Armory was not established in Springfield until 1794.

Oliver Iron Works In Middleborough

he earliest industries in Middleborough were grist and saw mills, followed by forges, furnaces, cotton mills, iron and shovel works. The largest and most important iron works were those owned and operated by Peter Oliver.

In 1744, Peter Oliver, a Chief Justice and a Loyalist, bought land at Muttock, including a dam and water privilege on the Nemasket River, and proceeded to build a forge and furnace.

Called the Olive Iron Works, they manufactured all kinds of iron ware. Oliver was an astute and aggressive business man and wanted to improve his business by incorporating a slitting and rolling mill to his works.

At that time the slitting process was a closely guarded secret, known in this country only to the Braintree and Saugus plants. To find out how it was done Judge Oliver hired a Hushai Thomas, knowledgeable and skilled in machinery, and, for a certain sum of money, persuaded Thomas to get a job as a laborer at the Braintree mill. There he was to observe the process and learn the art of "slitting".

When Thomas reported to Oliver the processes and equipment he had observed, he was placed in charge of the operation. Machinery was purchased and work begun at the Middleborough foundry.

With this addition, the Oliver Works became an active rival of the Braintree plant, and Muttock the most prosperous village in the town.

Because of his loyalty to King George, Oliver was able to secure large contracts from the Crown to furnish cannon, mortar, howitzers, shot and shell to be used in this country and abroad. At the beginning of the Revolutionary War, Oliver was staunchly supportive of the King and was supplying British troops with cannon and ammunition to be used against his compatriots.

The majority of the inhabitants in the area were Federalists and feeling against the Tories ran high. Although Judge Oliver had done a great deal for the town of Middleborough and its people, he was impeached for receiving a salary from the Crown. He left for Boston under the protection of British troops. A few days later Peter Oliver and his family joined Governor Gage and embarked for England, never to return.

In 1778, by an act of the Legislature, Oliver's land, home and business holdings were confiscated and sold. The works were managed by several owners and then purchased by General Abiel Washburn. Washburn and his son, Philander, manufactured shovels, making a successful and profitable business for themselves and the town.

Iron Works
At Taunton

lthough the Pilgrim fathers, Edward Winslow and Thomas Hopkins, had reconnoitered Cohannet, meaning "Place of Snow" in Indian language, and now called Taunton, the first white settlement there was not established until 1637.

A trading post was set up soon after the landing of the Pilgrims on the Teticutt, the Indian name meaning "Great River", but it remained uninhabited by white men until a group of forty-six Englishmen purchased a tract of land from the Neponset sachem. They actually paid for it twice as Massasoit made a conflicting claim.

Among the purchasers was William Pool, son of Sir William Pool, a noted antiquary. Although there is no record of the younger William Pool settling in Cohannet, his sister, Elizabeth, a maiden lady and forty-eight years old at the time, arrived in Dorchester in 1638 and set out soon after to establish a home in the country. She traveled through the wilderness with a sizable household which included servants, domestic animals, furniture and some farm equipment. In her entourage were a preacher, William Hooke, and a teacher, Nicholas Street.

Elizabeth's wealth and her claim were important enough to warrant attention from the Court and, in 1639, Captain Myles Standish and John Brown were sent to lay off fifty acres of "such upland as Miss Pool should choose". The following year they were instructed to define the boundaries of the town of Taunton, (so named for the English Taunton from which several of the inhabitants had come).

Miss Pool was particularly interested in the iron manufactory which some new arrivals, the Leonard brothers, proposed to construct. When the Taunton Iron Works were set up she supported them, both by investing in shares and encouraging others to do so.

Elizabeth Pool died in 1654, her epitaph describing her as a "general example of enterprise and of piety", and "a great proprietor of the township and a chief promoter of its settlement".

The iron works at Saugus did not have the support of the local citizenry due to fear of the depletion of the forests in the area. There was no such fear in the southeastern part of the Colony. The swamps and ponds were plentifully stocked with bog iron ore, the forests were dense and seemingly boundless, and Two Mile River could furnish water power. All was conducive to setting up an iron works on the banks of Two Mile River in that part of Taunton now known as Raynham.

James and Henry Leonard, from Pontipool, South Wales, and Ralph Russell, formerly connected with the Saugus and Braintree works, formed a stock company and built the Taunton Iron Works with a capital of 600 pounds. Opened in 1652, it was the first iron works in the Old Colony.

They were so successful that iron bars from their mill were as good as sterling pounds and became currency; taxes, school teachers' and ministers' salaries were paid with "iron money". It was claimed, locally, "Where you find iron works, there you will find a Leonard".

46

Later, Henry went to New Jersey and set up in the same business; Russell moved to Dartmouth. James remained in the original plant in Taunton.

It is interesting to note that Leonards of the old stock, through seven generations, had been engaged in the Taunton-Raynham works when the plant closed around 1880. Eliphalet, a fifth generation Leonard, operated an iron works in Easton and in the opening year of the Revolution, made the first bar of American steel. His son, Jonathan, was still making steel in Canton in 1826.

With the three prerequisites necessary for successful iron works plentiful in the Taunton area, several mills were established. The second was the Whittington Forge.

In 1666, James Leonard, Sr., who had been connected with the Taunton Iron Works, purchased ten acres of land with water privilege on Mill River and set up a "forge or bloomerie with one hearth". (It was located on the present site of Whittenton Mill Company). His sons Joseph, Benjamin and Uriah joined him and records show they were still operating it in 1678. They also built and operated a grist mill at this site.

After that, the business passed through several hands. In 1805, Samuel Crocker, Thomas Bush and Charles Richmond, who had been assistant clerks at Whittington and Hopewell, leased the water power and bought the grist mill at Whittington. In 1810 they built a nail factory where the nails were cut by crude machines, and the nail heads put on by hand.

Joseph Leonard, one of James' grandsons, carried on the early iron works at Two Mile River, but due to the increased cost of charcoal, a decreasing amount of good ore, and growing competition, he sold the controlling interest, about 1772, to Josiah Dean.

Dean converted the bar iron forge into a rolling mill and nail works and made copper bolts for ship builders. When his son, Major Elihab B. Dean, inherited the business in 1825, he changed the nail works into a forge and manufactured anchors. These works became a part of Raynham when Taunton was divided in 1731.

In 1695, Thomas and James Leonard found a suitable location for an iron works on the "North Purchase" in Taunton and bought it. The agreement stated that the proprietors did "deed and grant two lots of land of 100 acres each, next to Stoney Brook running into Coweeset River" for the purpose of building iron works and the privilege "to dig ore anywhere in the vicinity at 1s. per ton".

The resulting Chartley Iron Works, built in 1696-1707, were located in the west part of Taunton which is now Norton. The iron work and tools needed to construct the works were made at the Taunton Iron Works.

Captain James Leonard sold his half interest to his nephew George who, in 1713, received the other half by will at the death of his father, Captain Thomas Leonard. George made extensive additions to the plant and added nearly 1000 acres to his holdings.

Captain Zephaniah Leonard, who had been a forgeman in the old Taunton Iron Works for thirty years under Deacon Samuel Leonard's management, had a misunderstanding with the Deacon which resulted in a "friendly lawsuit" and the loss of his position.

Zephaniah bought part of an old saw mill from Jonathan and Joseph Barney with privileges on Mill River and, in 1739-40, built a forge for the manufacture of "charcoal iron", calling it Hopewell Iron Works.

He became a judge of the Court of Common Pleas in 1761, and made his home in Raynham.

The first hollow-ware made in the Old Colony was at King's Furnace in East Taunton. This furnace was located on Littleworth Brook and built, in 1723-24, by a joint stock company. The ore was obtained from the bogs bordering on the Littleworth and Taunton Rivers.

It has been related that the blast often lasted five or six months when "the workmen knew no regular days, nights, or Sundays; they bunked, alternately, in a furnace ante-room; the table was set standing in the cook-house day and night and the cooks on hand to serve".

The advertisements of the King's Furnace plant claimed that they manufactured hollow-ware from a "small jobie kettle to a ten pail cauldron".

General Cromwell Washburn and Colonel Nathan King rebuilt the furnace in 1816 and employed about thirty moulders and laborers. They not only supplied the surrounding countryside with hollow-ware, they also sent ware to New York on sloops berthed at Weir Village.

By this time it was necessary to import material for manufacturing their products. On their return trip, the sloops carried pig-iron and ore from New Jersey. Mixed with locally procured ore, a durable, non-brittle ware was produced.

The forge on Three Mile River was built by Richard Stephens in 1696. After his death Bollan and Laughton, wealthy English merchants of Boston, purchased a portion and leased the remaining interest belonging to Stephens' sons. The partners enlarged the works and, in 1739, contracted with Thomas Baylies, Jr., an iron master from London, to manage it. It later became known as the Baylies Iron Works.

At his death in 1756, Thomas' brother, Nicholas, came from Uxbridge and contracted with Bollan and Laughton to carry on an extensive forge business, manufacturing anchors, chains and other equipment for vessels, as well as farm implements.

Mr. Bollan and Mr. Laughton were Loyalists, and, as in all such cases, their holdings were confiscated in 1776 by the Commissioners of the Commonwealth, Captain Israel Washburn of Raynham, Captain Henry Hodges of Taunton, and Judge Samuel Tobey of Berkley.

Nicholas Baylies, however, was a firm supporter of the American cause and managed to save the works. He was a member of the Massachusetts Legislature in 1781-82, and again in 1786-87. Upon his death in 1807 he was succeeded at the plant by his son, Hodijah, and the Baylies Works were enlarged.

The frigate "Constitution" was supplied with several anchors during her active years and one of the anchors was made at the Bayliss Iron Works. It is said that it was so large that it took ten yoke of oxen to transport it to tide water in Dighton where it was loaded on board ship.

49

John Adams was a merchant in Taunton when he decided to enter the popular and profitable iron manufacturing business. In 1776-77 he erected a rolling and slitting mill near the Hopewell Works and on the same dam on Mill River in the northern section of Taunton. It was purchased in 1782 by Josiah Dean and Samuel Leonard who continued the business for about thirty years.

There was a fulling mill, a grist mill, and a saw mill a short distance above the Adams and Leonard iron works. All were finally owned by Horatio and Gustavus Leonard. Later the Reed and Barton Britannia Works was erected in their place.

Many smaller iron works were erected in the Taunton-Raynham area, ran for a short time and failed, or were incorporated into larger manufactories. The story of iron-making in Taunton is representative of the many successful industries built by men with foresight and perseverance that went into the building of America.

As iron ore, plentiful and with high iron content, was discovered by settlers moving westward, the great steel industry arose in the Lake Superior region of Minnesota and Michigan.

With the resultant decline of iron manufacturing in the East there began a search for industries to take its place. In southeastern Massachusetts the logical one was the cranberry industry. With peat and iron bogs already established, a plentiful water supply, and proper cultivation, "Cape Cod" cranberries were ready to enter the industrial world.

Cape Cod Cranberries

The Cranberry bogs appear as trim rectangular clearings bordered by purpling beach plums and the silvery bayberry. You see them everywhere on Cape Cod; snuggled under the leeward side of a sand dune, skirting a brook, tucked in the curve of a highway, or lying beside a quiet pond.

Geologists have concluded that the Ice Age, which ended 20,000 years ago, deposited a tongue of ice called the Buzzards Bay Glacier. This glacier filled Buzzards Bay to the Elizabeth Islands. Another field of ice, the Cape Cod Glacier, filled Massachusetts Bay. A sand bar was deposited between them which became Cape Cod.

The glaciers also molded the topography of the land, creating courses for streams, locations for ponds, future swamps, iron bogs and peat beds. This area became the cradle of the cranberry.

The cranberry, whose botanical name is Vaccinum Macrocarpon, is considered a native North American fruit and indigenous to Cape Cod. It is a small red acid berry which grows in bogs and marshes on slender upright branches of ground-hugging evergreen shrubs. Although similar berries grew in many of the swamp areas of northern Asian and central European countries, they were inferior in size and flavor to those grown in America. The European berry, when ripe, is globular and little more than one-quarter inch in diameter. Since it grows in low marshy land or on peat bogs, it is called moss berry, or moor berry, in some localities.

The European moss berry was almost exclusively a northern plant and was probably not known to the Romans until their conquests in the North. It has been used for food and drink since ancient times, however. Indeed, a Bronze Age tomb near Egtved, Jutland, in Denmark, yielded a clay mug in which there remained a brown sediment. Analysis showed that it was the remains of a wine containing wheat, cranberries, bog myrtle and honey.

The tart, brilliantly red berry, produced for centuries in Russia and Sweden, was a novelty to inhabitants in Great Britain and demanded high prices when brought into the English market annually.

In America these low-trailing, berry-producing evergreen shrubs were found growing between the beach plum and bayberry bushes by the Pilgrims. It is believed that the early name for the plant was Craneberry because the tiny, bell-shaped flowers, drooping on their slender stalks, resembled the head and neck of the crane, a cousin of the blue heron. The ripe berries were also a favorite food of the long-legged birds which waded and fed in the marshes.

The native American cranberry is larger, juicier and more flavorful than its European counterpart. The fruit has a smooth skin, is generally round, elliptical or bell-shaped, about one-third inch in diameter and one-half to one inch long. Inconspicuous seeds are attached at the center of the berry and surrounded by tart pulp.

The Cape Cod cranberry has had a distinct and favorable heritage which has rendered succeeding generations productive and disease resistant. All the most valuable and reliable cultivated varieties of the present day plants belong to this sub-species or are hybrids of it.

A charming folk story is told in the booklet "Cranberries, America's Native Fruit" published by Ocean Spray, which tells how cranberries came to grow on Cape Cod.

The Reverend Richard Bourne, a preacher and early settler on Cape Cod, had an argument with an Indian medicine man, presumably a religious one regarding the powers of each. To prove his superiority, the angry "pow wow" cast a spell and mired Bourne's feet in quicksand so that he couldn't move.

After much shouting and dickering it was agreed that the Reverend would be freed if he could best his opponent in a battle of wits. In the ensuing fifteen days weighty problems and mind teasing questions and answers were exchanged with neither man winning the battle.

During the time that he was trapped in the sand Reverend Bourne was nourished and kept alive by a white dove who placed a succulent red berry in his mouth from time to time.

The medicine man watched the dove's lifesaving ministrations to his opponent but was unable to cast a spell to prevent it. Finally, exhausted from his own lack of food and water, the Indian medicine man fell to the ground and Bourne was set free.

On the frequent trips that the dove made, ministering to the Reverend, several berries fell to the ground. Finding root in the bog, they grew and multiplied, and that was the beginning of cranberries on Cape Cod.

There are three essentials for the successful culture of cranberries: (1) a swampy flat or bog with a firm base and a fresh water supply close by for flooding; (2) suitable sand; and (3) a long growing season without killing frosts. In the early days Cape Cod met these requirements. Unsuitable for anything else, the bog lands were present; the sea breezes blew loose beach sand over the shrubs; the warmth of the nearby ocean tempered frosts and protected the plants and the fruit. These essentials were "accidental" discoveries but proved to be invaluable in the cultivation of cranberries.

When we discuss Cape Cod cranberries in present day cultivation we include all cranberries grown in southeastern Massachusetts, as the term "Cape Cod" has become synonymous with area produced cranberries.

Early Uses of
The Cranberry

o other fruit or berry is so representative of America and all she stands for as the native cranberry. The Pilgrims found these little "waifs of the swampland" growing wild in the marshes when they stepped ashore at Truro on Cape Cod, and again at Plymouth.

Colorful accounts of the first Thanksgiving in the fall of 1621 relate that cranberries were served along with wild turkey, succotash, squash and cornbread when the Pilgrims and their Indian guests gathered around the long pineboard table.

Long before the Pilgrims landed at Plymouth Rock, however, cranberries had been used as life saving food and medicine. In 1550, James White Norwood's diary makes reference to Indians using cranberries. In James Rosier's book "The Land of Virginia", printed in England in 1605, he tells of coming ashore and being presented with birchbark cups of berries.

Roger Williams wrote "Key Into The Language" in 1640, and described cranberries, calling them "bearberries" because bears ate them.

The Indians used the tart marsh berries, which they called "sassamanesh", in various ways. Picked green, roasted and mashed into a poultice, they believed that the mixture had the power to draw out the venom from a poisoned-arrow wound. Mixed with deer fat and meal the ripe red berries gave pemmican cakes flavor and appeal. Cooked with corn and beans, it became a favorite dish called "succotash".

Among the many lifesaving things taught by the Indians to their new neighbors was the preservation and use of the wild fruits and berries growing so abundantly in the woods, fields and marshes. They showed the Pilgrims how to harvest, dry and store the native fruits, vegetables and nuts. Of course, among these were the wild cranberry. The Pilgrim Cook Book, appearing in 1663, described cranberry sauce.

John Josselyn wrote a book in 1672, "New England Rarities Discovered", in which he described "Sauce For The Pilgrims — Cranberry or Bearberry, (because the Bears use much to feed upon them) is a small trayling plant that grows in salt marshes that are overgrown with moss. The berries are a pale yellow color, afterwards red, as big as a cherry, some perfectly round, others oval, all of them hollow with sower astringent taste; they are ripe in August and September. They are excellent against the Scurvy. They are also good to allay the fervor of hoof-Diseases.

The Indians and English use them much, boyling them with sugar for Sauce to eat with their meat; and it is a delicate Sauce, especially with Roasted Mutton. Some make tarts with them as with Gooseberries."

On the auspicious occasion when Captain Richard Cobb took his second wife, Mary Gorham, the daughter of Mayor Gorham of Yarmouth, and also to celebrate his election as representative to the Convention of Assistance, he had a banquet at his home at which sauce from wild cranberries was served with turkey. To commemorate the double event a notch was carved in the beam of their home, which can still be seen.

Cranberries were considered such a delicacy and so superior in quality and taste to the European species that the Colonists, in 1677, sent ten barrels of cranberries "along with two hogsheads of semp [cracked Indian corn], and 3000 codfish" to King Charles II to appease him for the coining of the Pine Tree shilling.

As sugar, molasses and maple syrup became more readily available, the Pilgrim and Puritan women, with their English tastes and preference for preserved and stewed fruit, were soon inventing cranberry sauce, tarts, shrub, and nog.

The recipe for a shrub was published in the Compleat Cook's Guide, in 1683, which read: "Put a teacupful of cranberries into a cup of water and mash them. In the meantime, boil two quarts and a pint of water with one large spoonful of oatmeal and a very large bit of lemon. Then add the cranberries and as much fine Lisbon sugar as shall leave a smart."

The health-giving qualities of these marsh-grown berries were soon recognized and, as trading with other countries increased and longer voyages were undertaken by New England ships, barrels of cranberries, packed in spring water, were included in the supplies stored in the hold. Served to the sailors as part of their diet, they were thought to ward off scurvy, one of the most dreaded diseases aboard ship. In the same manner that English "limeys" ate limes, American sailors ate cranberries to counteract a Vitamin C deficiency.

In the opening of the West scurvy was also a problem in the logging camps; cranberries, found growing wild, were added to the loggers' rations.

Cranberries are mentioned in the diaries kept by the members of the Lewis and Clark expedition in the exploration of the Northwest Territory. When they reached the lower Columbia River the explorers found cranberries growing on the Clatsop Plain and bought supplies of them from the Indians.

Contrary to present-day belief, the English liked bright colors, and soon after building their homes and laying by provisions of food, were following the Indians' example of dying wool, yarn, and pieces of cloth to be used for patchwork quilts with the juices of red and yellow fruits and berries.

When Mary Ring died in Plymouth in 1633 her petticoat was auctioned by her husband for sixteen shillings because it was "wondrously dyed" with cranberries.

In spite of the abundance of cranberries in the Plymouth area and on Cape Cod, it was nearly 200 years before cultivation was attempted. Even then, the berries were grown only for home and local consumption.

Beginning of Cranberry Cultivation

he great cranberry industry had its beginning on Cape Cod. A patch of wild cranberries, snuggled behind a protective sand dune in North Dennis, gave the first hint of successful cultivation.

About the year 1816 Henry Hall, a Revolutionary War veteran, cut some small timber on a knoll near land on which wild cranberries grew. The removal of the brush permitted sand to blow over the vines, nearly burying them, and Hall fully expected that they would die. Instead of being suffocated or injured, the plants sprang up through the covering of sand and seemed to thrive. They produced more and larger berries. In his "History of Barnstable County" Deyo calls this incident "an accidental discovery". This was the origin of successful cranberry cultivation.

In East Dennis Elkanah Sears, also a veteran of the Revolution, and his son William, noted Hall's thriving vines and set out some plants in an area where they would receive the benefit of the drifting sand, growing fruit for their own use. In 1840 Isaiah Baker decided to "set a few rods to cranberries" in the neighboring town of West Harwich.

The practice caught on. In 1845 Captain Alvan Cahoon, then sailing a vessel out of North Dennis, noticed Hall's sturdy, productive plants as he passed by on his way to the harbor and "set out eight rods to berries" at Pleasant Lake in Harwich.

Cahoon's neighbors scoffed and belittled his modest attempt to cultivate the wild cranberry, but when they saw the resultant product, recognized the possibilities and hastened to turn their own idle waste land into cranberry bogs. Mr. Cahoon lived to see the growth of the cranberry market expand and become world-wide in its distribution.

About this same time Zebina H. Small started a plot at Grassy Pond but it was not successful and he lost his $400.00 investment. On the other hand, Nathaniel Robbins, of Harwich, started a bog in 1852 and became an extensive grower. Jonathan Small sanded a bog at South Harwich, known as Deep Hole Bog. Deacon Braley Jenkins of West Barnstable cultivated a bog at Sandy Neck.

These men were the leaders, and these dates mark the period from which the culture of cranberries may be dated in Barnstable County.

For over one hundred years the cranberry industry in Dennis and Harwich was carried on by former sea captains whose names were Atwood, Doane, Hawes, Nickerson, Sears, names as familiar in Hong Kong as they were on Cape Cod.

The pioneer in the cranberry business in Bourne was Seth Maxim, who, about the middle of the nineteenth century, built a bog near his home and bought his vines from his home town of Carver.

Other Bourne men who began cultivating "the little waif of the swampland" were Captain Ellis Swift, Captain Russell Blackwell, the Phinneys, David Ellis, Moses and Abraham Keene. All of their bogs were located in the Old Run Swamp.

By 1854 cranberry growing had become important enough to warrant an official census. The "Abstract", compiled by the Massachusetts Department of Agriculture, showed the number of cranberry-producing acres, value of crop, value of crop per acre, and value of land per acre. This information is still compiled and released periodically.

In the 1855 census there were 197 acres in Barnstable County under cranberry cultivation: Dennis had 50, Barnstable 33, Falmouth 26, Provincetown 25, Brewster 21, Harwich 17, Orleans 8, Eastham, Sandwich and Yarmouth had 5 each, Wellfleet 2. By 1865 the census showed 1074 acres in the county with Harwich leading with 209 acres.

The first cranberry historian was Reverend Benjamin Eastwood who wrote "The Complete Manual for the Cultivation of the Cranberry", published in 1856.

Quoting from Reverend Eastwood's account of cranberry growing and marketing: "Every year the cranberry is in greater demand. — It is becoming a staple article in the great markets of the country", and "The American cranberry is coming into notice in Europe, but most especially in England. It is sold there in small bottles into which the fruit is first put, and then filled with water and hermetically sealed. We have seen 'Cape Cod Bell Cranberry' sold at four shillings sterling in the Strand, London."

This book came to the attention of farmers in New Jersey where agricultural requirements seemed similar. Large quantities of vines were sent from Massachusetts to start the cultivation of cranberries there.

Although the vicinity of Duxbury was described as "A whole countrie full of woods and thickets" by Governor William Bradford, the early settlers, among whom were Captain Myles Standish, John Alden, John Bradford, Samuel Nash and Constant Southworth, were careful to mark for protection the wild fruits and berries that the Indians had taught them to use. Among these were the cranberries, growing so plentifully in the low swampy areas. The berries were used solely for home consumption, however, and cultivation for commercial purposes was not undertaken for more than two hundred years; not until they heard of the remunerative results of the experiments on the Cape.

About 1845-46 Stephen Gifford decided to try his hand at raising cranberries commercially. His neighbor, John Loring, tried cultivating them, while the Fletcher bog began to pay dividends. According to "The Story Of Duxbury — 1637-1937" edited by E. Waldo Long, a bog was still in operation in 1937 which was built by Joseph Weston in 1872.

At the time of the Duxbury Tercentenary there were about 600 acres of cranberry bogs, operated by twenty-five people, which were producing an average crop of 36,000 bushels with an estimated value of $120,000.00.

Although cranberries grew wild in Colonial times, the same problems arose concerning the rights of individuals as had arisen concerning the digging of iron ore. To whom did the product belong, and if it were on public land, what restrictions should be issued?

In Plymouth County and on Cape Cod a law was established that the people might not pick cranberries before the crop was fully ripe, generally September 20th, and anyone so doing was subject to a fine. As early as 1773 a Cape Cod town clerk recorded that anyone picking more than a quart of cranberries before the 20th of September would be fined one dollar, in addition to having to forfeit the berries.

In Wisconsin, where Indians and white people alike harvested the fruit in the wild marshes, a law provided a penalty of $50.00 for picking or having in one's possession unripe berries before September 20th. New Jersey had a similar law, enacted in 1789, preventing cranberry picking before October 10th; the fine being 10 shillings.

Building A Bog

In Cape Cod the production of cranberries was a natural outgrowth of the ever present need to earn a living. Through the years various industries had flourished and declined; salt-making, glass making, farming, fishing, and trading via the sea. As they died out it was necessary to find other commercial ventures to replace them.

Former sea captains and fishermen who wished to retire from the sea and who owned several acres of marshland found cranberry raising easily managed and profitable once the initial work was done.

Cranberries are grown in bogs especially made for them. The plants require special conditions of moisture, soil structure, and acidity. It is interesting to follow the steps taken in preparing and establishing such a bog.

An important prerequisite is the selction of a cedar or peat swamp or an old iron bog near a stream or body of fresh water large enough to flood and drain the area.

Water is needed during the summer months when the rainfall is insufficient. The normal requirement of cranberry vines is one inch a week. When not supplied by normal rainfall the plot is irrigated by filling ditches constructed for that purpose and allowing the water to soak into the soil. This is called "flash flooding", — flooding the entire surface and then drawing off the water as quickly as possible. Overhead sprinkler systems have been used recently by some bog owners, proving to be a more efficient, but expensive method of maintaining the proper amount of moisture in the bog.

Old iron bogs make an excellent foundation for cranberry bogs as they have the necessary moisture, a firm base, and acid soil. Mr. Bartholomew, owner of the Edaville Railroad in Carver, tells me that evidence of iron ore in the soil is manifested regularly in the maintenance of the ditches around the bogs by the tell-tale reddish-brown color of the earth.

The builder reclaims the swampland by clearing out all trees, stumps, brush and undergrowth, and leveling off the area. A narrow ditch is dug around the edge of the plot so that surface water may be drained off. The earth thus thrown out forms an embankment which restricts the overflow and contains the water in the flooded section for protection in times of frost.

Sometimes it is necessary to remove the top soil of the swamp to reach a sufficiently firm base for the planting. This topsoil makes excellent fertilizer. When the floor is level and firm a layer of sand, about three inches deep, is spread over the surface, more if the soil is loose and pliant. Sand prevents weeds from growing, keeps the berries clean, and prevents the peat base in which the roots grow from drying out.

The size of the bed is immaterial, although on large areas a long narrow plot is easier to spray, cultivate and pick. It is also more economical since the workers do not have so far to travel in attending the plants and in harvesting. The necessary ingredients are a uniform depth of sand and proper moisture.

In the spring cuttings from preferred vines are set out deep enough so that the roots will take hold in the soil below the sand. The plants are spaced about six inches apart and in rows eighteen inches to four feet apart, depending on the quantity and quality of the plants. Cranberry vines are similar to strawberry plants, sending out tendrils which grow roots and spread. The trailing vines have many slender upright branches. It is these uprights that bear the flowers and fruit.

In planting, the object is to cover the entire surface of the bog with vines as quickly as possible. The better the plant, the sooner this will be accomplished. In three or four years the whole area will be covered and ready to produce the first crop. The first productive year often repays the owner for his initial investment and the cost of the labor up to that time.

It is necessary to cultivate a new bog carefully until the plants are firmly established and have covered the entire surface, preventing weeds and underground roots from springing up. Weeding is still done by hand, particularly of poison ivy which has a tendency to creep in among the vines. Individuals who are immune to the ivy are especially sought to help in the removal of ivy and receive a bonus beyond the regular salary.

Once a bog is established little cultivation is required. With care a properly planted and maintained cranberry bog will bear fruit indefinitely and produce a steady income for the owner.

In the early years the bogs on Cape Cod were cared for by members of the family. The men cleared the land and sanded it; the women set out the plants and weeded. At harvest time men, women and children gathered the berries, screened them and prepared them for market. In those days an average yield was fifty barrels to an acre; wholesale prices ranged from $8.00 to $15.00 a barrel. A five acre bog provided all the necessities and a few extras for a family, while a ten acre bog kept its owners in comparative luxury.

The story is told of a native Cape Codder who harvested ten barrels of cranberries and loaded them on his wagon one bright September morning. Horse-drawn, the cart was piloted over the sandy Harwich roads to Brewster where the barrels were placed on a packet bound for Boston. The grower, a retired sea captain, returned to his homeplace in the late afternoon the richer by ten twenty-dollar gold pieces.

The Life Cycle
of A Cranberry

The cranberry thrives best where the summers are relatively cool. Cuttings pruned from a bog with a good production record are planted either in the spring or in the fall. In any case the plants must be protected from freezing in the winter. To accomplish this the bog is flooded with fresh water and frozen to a depth of eight inches. The water underneath this protective layer of ice is drained off so that the plants can "breathe".

Young skaters who live near a cranberry bog watch eagerly for the first "freeze" for they know that the ice on a bog makes the best possible skating rink. Snow must not be permitted to accumulate on the ice, for light must penetrate to the "resting" plants below and continue the photosynthetic activity of the vines.

In the spring, usually about April 1st, the flume boards are raised and the water is drained off. A few days of sun, and the reddish-brown leaves, dormant through the winter months, again turn green and send out runners of the season's new growth.

Insecticides and fungicides are used in cranberry cultivation, but they differ according to the various requirements of the individual bogs. They must be non-toxic to bees and swallows, for these living creatures are also necessary to cranberry growth.

Many Massachusetts owners erect bird houses, built to specifications of swallow likes and dislikes, to encourage these little feathered tenants to remain near the bog. A swallow eats his weight in insects every day and thus becomes a valuable asset in the growth of cranberries. His arrival in the spring is timed with the draining of the bog, and his departure with harvest time and the cool fall air.

June and July is blossom time. The pale pink flowers, nodding on their slender stems, give the appearance of a field lightly dusted with powder. Many growers rent hives of honey bees and set them along the bog's edge to promote pollination and a good crop. A 1967 study in Massachusetts showed that 289 growers who used bees reported an average yield of 7400 pounds of berries per acre, while 340 growers who did not set out bee hives averaged 5300 pounds per acre.

Of the many "faces" of a cranberry bog, harvest time is the most colorful. Along about Labor Day the leaves of the plant, as well as the berries, triggered by near-frosty nights and warm Indian summer days, turn a bright red, giving the area the effect of a huge patchwork quilt.

In Massachusetts harvesting sometimes starts in early September, beginning with the Early Blacks, and continuing through October with later ripening varieties.

The piquant little red berry, once called "the waif of the swamplands", has provided, over the years, one of Cape Cod's most picturesque and fascinating activities. Even at the present time, when harvesting is done with machinery, it is still interesting to watch.

In the early days "picking time" was festival time. Like the "husking bees" and "barn raisings" all other work was put aside until the cranberry crop had been harvested.

In many communities school was dismissed to permit the children to assist in picking the fruit. In 1872 the Provincetown school master wrote in the Town Report: "35 permits were granted to absentees—a large proportion cranberry pickers. Some parents felt the need of assistance of all their children."

Although it was not until 1847 that the Harwich captain, Cyrus Cahoon, first made a commercial success of his cranberry bog, the state census shows that, in 1855, Falmouth already had 26 acres under cultivation. As late as 1927 it was apparent that all hands were needed in harvesting, as evidenced by the fact that, on November 5, four parents in Falmouth were brought into court, charged with keeping their minor children out of school, and as defense, produced permits from the Superintendent of Schools to allow their children to be absent for the purpose of picking cranberries.

A colorful description of cranberry pickers was written by Geneva Eldridge in the July 1915 edition of the Cape Cod Magazine: "And stretching itself like some lazy snake in the sun, the old sandy road wound in and out and over the long hill that led to Skaket Cranberry Bog. I stood on the side of the road, waiting for the cart to come along that would carry me to the bog for the day's picking.

Uncle Ez Higgins was the driver, an old sea captain, who had brought many a catch from the Grand Banks and in early life had twice rounded the Horn. He drove the horse, old Fan, much as he would sail a ship. In fact, Uncle Ez's conversation was carried on in a nautical strain and furnished much amusement to the boys and girls.

All the women wore sun bonnets that covered their faces from the sun's gleaming rays. Big blue denim aprons with a patch of oil cloth across the front enveloped them from the waistline to their toes. The oil cloth came under their knees when they knelt to pick and, if the bog was wet, kept them dry. On their fingers were stalls made of white cloth, and over these were drawn mitts made of cast-off stocking legs. These were to prevent them from the sharp vines. Everybody carried a tin six quart measure, their lunch and the inevitable bottle of tea."

Pickers were paid ten cents for a heaping measure. Many young people bought their own school clothes and shoes by picking cranberries, and were proud to say they had earned the money for them.

Homemade scoops followed handpicking. Made of wood, the long curved teeth combed through the vines and collected the berries which dropped down into the scoop. In the beginning each scoop was about 12 to 15 inches wide and held about two quarts of berries, but later were made as large as 22 and 24 inches.

Long lines of cord were drawn across the bog with two people to a lane. The pickers moved along the aisles, scooping the berries. As the scoop was filled it was emptied into bushel boxes placed at intervals throughout the bog. The boxes had slits on the sides and bottoms for ventilation. Each box held five measures and the picker was paid forty cents per box.

When the boxes were full they were picked up and taken to the screening shed for sorting and grading, and emptied into 100 pound barrels. Carted to railroad freight stations or steamship piers, the barrels were shipped to commission merchants in Boston and New York.

Beginning of
Cranberry Industry

p to the time of the Civil War there was a slow but steady increase in acreage turned over to cranberry cultivation on Cape Cod, but the berries were still used only for home and local consumption.

After the war an industrial depression took place which had a far-reaching effect on the cranberry industry. The depression was due to three factors: (1) the replacement of wooden sailing ships by iron steamships; (2) shipping by rail instead of by sea; and (3) the decline of the fisheries.

With the decline of ship building and the fishing industry, cranberry production proved to be the salvation of the Cape. Captains and fishermen who owned bogs and marshes (until then practically valueless land) cleared and drained them, and set out cranberry vines. The resultant production and sale of the fruit provided a welcome income to families who had been struggling with poverty, and to widows who were surprised and grateful recipients of a few hundred dollars on a deceased husband's investment.

At this point, also, a new process for manufacturing white sugar made it sufficiently cheap to warrant general use, and by making the cranberry more palatable, contributed to the growth of the cranberry industry. Whole families, furnished with employment and ready cash, found themselves suddenly financially independent.

Cape Cod sentiment of that time is expressed in the poem "Attune" by "Cap'n Bill":

> "There's nothing to me in foreign lands
> like the stuff that grows in Cape Cod sands;
> there's nothing in sailing of foreign seas
> equal to getting down on your knees
> and pulling the pizen ivy out.
> I guess I knew what I was about
> when I put by my chart and glass,
> and took to growing cranberry sass."

(Taken from "Cranberry and Reunion Week at East Dennis, Massachusetts — July 23–July 30, 1933.)

In the days of ship building the financing of a vessel was accomplished by selling 1/64th interests. Bog-building for cranberries was expensive; thus when these retired sea captains wished to finance their bogs, they resorted to the method used in financing their ships and sold 64th interests. To this day there are cranberry bogs on Cape Cod from which some thirty or forty stockholders receive dividends, heirs of early investors who bought one, two, or more "64ths" when the bogs were built.

A modern example of this old time practice in financing is the part ownership of the well-known radio and television personality, Arthur Godfrey. He is a one-fourth owner of twenty-five acres of cranberry bogs in Carver, Massachusetts, formerly owned by Trufant Cranberry Company. Other owners of a fourth are an executive of the national cooperative, Ocean Spray Cranberries, Inc., a Wareham cranberry grower, and an executive of H. P. Hood Company. This holding is called Godfrey Cranberry Company, and makes Arthur a grower-member of the cooperative.

Up to about the time of the Civil War, there were three staple types of cranberries. They were probably named because of their shapes: (1) "Bugle", an elliptical berry, pointed at both ends; (2) "Cherry", round; and (3) "Bell", pear-shaped.

In developing the cranberry the most perfect vines were selected and grown under favorable conditions. The hybrids, or future varieties, were named, for the most part, for those men who produced them. The "Howes", according to Farmers' Bulletin #1400 of the United States Department of Agriculture, was propagated in 1843 by Eli Howes of East Dennis, and continued by his son, James Paine Howes. The "Smalley", a Bell type, was grown by James A. Smalley, about 1853, on his bog at Sesuit Neck, in East Dennis.

One exception was the "Early Black". About this same time Captain Nathaniel Robbins gave Captain Cyrus Cahoon some vines to plant on his land in Harwich. Early in the fall, a couple of years later, Lettice, Captain Cahoon's wife, noticed a different cranberry ripening in the bog. It was early in the season for cranberries to ripen and this berry was deep red, almost black in color. The bog was located on the floor of Black Pond and, all things considered, Mrs. Cahoon named her find "Early Black".

This berry, early on the market with good keeping qualities and excellent flavor, was actively promoted by the more prominent growers, including Abel D. Makepeace.

Abel D. Makepeace of Hyannis, and later of Wareham, owned several bogs in Barnstable County. He was considered to be the first Cape Cod man to recognize the potentialities and to foresee the success that the production and marketing of cranberries would achieve.

Realizing that the huge swamp area in Plymouth County afforded the opportunity to produce cranberries on a large scale, he invested his own money and persuaded his friends to invest in the development of this promising new industry.

Founder of the A. D. Makepeace Cranberry Company, a company still in existence at the present time, Abel D. Makepeace was given the title of "Cranberry King" when he became the largest cultivator in the country.

Sea captains, fishermen and shipbuilders took up cranberry cultivation in Barnstable County, but in Carver and Wareham men formerly associated with the iron industry were the visionaries of the great cranberry business.

Mr. George Bowers, an iron master in Carver, and Mr. John Russell, a banker in Plymouth, were the first pioneers on a large scale in Plymouth County. They chose an old marsh in Carver called Benson's Pond and set out their first cranberry vines.

In 1878 Mr. Bowers began the construction of East Head bog which became a model for other bogs and the most valuable in town. It had ideal sand, water and proper drainage. About this time A. D. Makepeace moved from Hyannis and began the development of a large swamp around Wankino which ultimately developed into the largest single tract bog in the state.

Other prominent growers in this area were Sampson McFarlin, Luther Atwood, Benjamin Finney, Joseph and Benjamin W. Robbins, John Dunham, George Shurtleff, Eben and Earl Sherman, P. W.

Berry, H. A. Lucas, Ephraim Griffith, Nathan Ryder, Nathaniel S. and Matthew H. Cushing, and Atwood Shaw. Peleg McFarlin, the last of the old iron masters in Carver, also cultivated cranberries extensively.

Thomas Huit McFarlin and his brother, Charles Dexter McFarlin, developed the McFarlin cranberry. Their home was near New Meadows marsh, a natural cranberry bog of over 500 acres. It was here that Charles Dexter built the "first cranberry laboratory bog" where he demonstrated how cranberries could be cultivated and produced in quantity under the right conditions. Growers throughout the state visited his "laboratory" and observed correct and rewarding experiments in proper cultivation.

McFarlin became restless, however, and decided to go West to pan for gold in California. This did not turn out as he anticipated and he turned again to cranberry cultivation. Planting Massachusetts vines, Charles Dexter set out the first cranberry bog in Oregon. Established in 1885 this bog is still bearing. From this first planting McFarlin developed a variety of berry adapted to the growing conditions on the Pacific Coast which still bears his name.

Distribution
of Cranberry Bogs

espite the fact that the harvested acreage of cranberries fell from 13,000 to 11,400 during the period 1960 to 1968, cranberry growers produced the four largest crops in the history of the industry. This leads one to conclude that modern technology has had a hand in increased production per acre.

According to a 1968 bulletin, "The Cranberry Industry in Massachusetts", compiled by Byron S. Peterson, Chester E. Cross and Nathaniel Tilden, this is due to: (1) Continued installation of solid-set sprinkler systems for frost protection, irrigation, and successful insect and disease control; (2) Conversion to flood harvest where possible; and (3) Daily application of the grower or operator to the year round problems of cranberry cultivation.

Up until the beginning of the twentieth century cranberry acreage was widely distributed throughout the Commonwealth. Middlesex County, cultivating about 2500 acres, was the leader. However, poor management and poorly engineered bogs led to its decline. Barnstable County took over the lead for a while but, around 1890, Plymouth County forged ahead and has remained in that position to the present day.

There are several reasons for this, but probably the most important are types of soil and the availability of water. Cranberries thrive on muck land (organic matter mixed with some mineral matter). Ponds, lakes and streams abound in southeastern Massachusetts. A United States Department of Agriculture survey shows that, between 1912 and 1924, Plymouth County accounted for 70,000 acres of muck land, with 3200 acres in Barnstable County.

The number of acres given over to cranberry cultivation in Barnstable County (Cape Cod) peaked about 1905, nearly 4700 acres, but has declined since then to the present level of about 1800 acres.

Contributing factors to this decline were several: earlier bogs constructed on poor soil types; no water flowage available; the topography of the land changed by a hurricane and salt water overtaking the location of some bogs; and, a big factor, the increase and monetary rewards of 'tourism'.

By 1915, over 95.5 per cent of Massachusetts cranberry acreage was located in the southeastern section (west of Cape Cod Canal) where there is an abundance of ponds, streams and lakes so necessary in the successful development and maintenance of cranberry bogs. The shift in acreage is shown by the fact that 70 towns had one or more acres of bog in 1846, but by 1966, the number was down to 54. At the present time the concentration of cranberry cultivation is in Plymouth County, with Carver the leader, followed by the towns of Wareham, Plymouth, and Middleborough, in that order. These four towns account for more than half of the state's cranberry producing acreage.

Cranberry bogs vary in size. On Cape Cod they may be as small as one-half acre and as large as sixty acres. In the more fertile areas of Carver, Wareham, Plymouth and Middleborough the sizes range from one to 200 acres.

Until recently the largest flooded cranberry bog (contained in one parcel) in the world was located on Nantucket Island. Upon the death of its former owner, some acreage was given for conservation, thus reducing the size of the cranberry-producing parcel.

A fascinating way to see a working cranberry bog is to board a coach on the Edaville Railroad, the historic narrow-gauge railroad, and ride the 5½ mile "iron horse trail". Winding through the 210 acres of cranberry bogs in New Meadows, the track skirts rusty-colored irrigation ditches, passing such points of interest as Rusty River, Rattelsnake Curve, Cranberry Valley, Mt. Urann, Sunset Vista, Wilderness Point Forests and Cranberry Harvest.

The dwarf-size engine, flat cars and coaches were purchased by Mr. and Mrs. Ellis D. Atwood in the early 1940's. In 1946, at the end of World War II, the separate units of the train were loaded onto wide-bed trucks and transported from Bridgeton, Maine to Edaville.

In the beginning it was used as a working train in the upkeep of the bogs and the collection of hundreds of boxes of cranberries during harvesting. Rides were generously offered to visitors interested in an active cranberry bog.

At Mr. Atwood's death, in 1950, the Edaville Railroad was leased and operated, not only as an educational experience, but as a tourist attraction. The Edaville bogs, like all cranberry bogs, present a different face at various times of the year; in the late spring, the blossoming vines appear to be sprinkled with myriads of pink and white confetti; during the summer months, the bog looks like a peaceful green meadow with creamy waxen berries growing and ripening under the summer sun; during September and October the bogs are vibrant and active with the harvesting of the brilliant red fruit; then comes the quiet time. Through the winter the vines are dormant under a blanket of ice and snow, and the stillness is broken only by the nostalgic sound of the steam engine's whistle as the little train chugs along the ribbon-like rails.

Cape Cod Cranberry Bogs

West Yarmouth
Bayview — Cape Cod Hospital
Old Colony — Thatcher

Dennis
Grassy Pond — Makepeace

Harwich
Dam Brook — Thatcher
Big OK — Thatcher
Little OK — Thatcher
Long Pond — L. Fernandes
Brown Bog — R. Crowell

Barnstable
Muddy Pond — Childs — Makepeace
Mystic Lake — Lampi & Waldo
San Juan — Taylor
Leman Bogs — Ames

Falmouth
John's Pond — Makepeace

Provincetown

East Dennis

Dennis

Yarmouth

Sandwich

Bourne

Barnstable

Harwich

Falmouth

Cape Cod Cranberry Growers' Association And Cranberry Experiment Station

The Cape Cod Cranberry Growers' Association was founded and held its first meeting on July 10, 1888 in Sandwich, Massachusetts. It was formed by a group of about forty growers from Barnstable and Plymouth Counties for the purpose of promoting "the interests of its members in whatever pertains to the growth, cultivation and sale of cranberries". Among those present and participating was Abel D. Makepeace, founder of the A. D. Makepeace Cranberry Company. The first president was John J. Russell of Plymouth. Mr. Makepeace was Vice-President.

Among the many accomplishments of the Association, two are outstanding: (1) being responsible for the legislation that created the Cranberry Experiment Station. and (2) the formation and sponsoring of the Frost Warning Service.

The Cape Cod Cranberry Growers' Association was responsible for bringing the need of an experimental station to the attention of the state. Pursuant to an act of the legislature, which provided a special appropriation for the purpose, a bog consisting of 12½ acres was purchased, and the Cranberry Station of the Agricultural Experiment Station, University of Massachusetts, was established in East Wareham in 1910.

Since that time the Station has investigated the culture, varieties, bog management, pest control, harvest, storage and other aspects of growing cranberries. As a related project they also study the culture of blueberries in the area. Several bulletins a year are issued covering these subjects and are available to growers.

The primary responsibility of the Cranberry Station is "to make science useful for the benefit of all citizens and the improvement of the agricultural industry".

The first director of the Cranberry Experiment Station (who was also recommended by the Cape Cod Cranberry Growers' Association) was the eminent biologist, Dr. H. J. Franklin. Under Dr. Franklin's guidance many far-reaching and beneficial experiments were conducted and the results tabulated for the growers' information.

The work has been continued since 1952 under the able direction of Dr. Chester E. Cross and continues to make valuable contributions to benefit the cranberry industry. Industry in general has also benefited greatly from the experimental work carried on at the Station.

It has been the general policy of the Cranberry Station to maintain as broad a program of cranberry research as possible, with special attention to experiments which yield practical results, at the same time keeping growers supplied with current information.

Aided in research by the United States Weather Bureau, the Bureau of Plant Industry, and County agencies, the various areas covered in their research are:

1. Injurious and beneficial insects affecting cranberries. Over a period of fifty-plus years most of the pests have been identified and measures taken to control them. It has also been established that the work of the bees as polenizers is necessary and effective.

2. Cranberry diseases, — what causes them and how to control them. Two important results were obtained in studying diseases, one being the discovery of the nature of false blossom disease and its control; the other, a method of testing the keeping qualities of cranberries in incubators, indicating where they should be sold at a given time.

3. Bog weeds and their eradication. The control of cranberry bog weeds by chemicals; some of this information applies to weed control in general.

4. Bog fertilizers. Tests of various fertilizer elements and their results.

5. Cranberry varieties. The botanical relationships of cranberry varieties and the correlations of fruit and vine characteristics with productiveness and disease resistance. Much crossing of selected

material has been carried out and the information reported to growers to assist them in making selections.

6. Cranberry weather relations. These include frost and frost prediction; relation of the weather to cranberry production, and relation of the weather during the growing season to the development of rot in fruit.

7. Cranberry storage. As a result of these studies it has been determined that cranberries keep best shipped in quarter-barrel boxes and cellophane bags. Through tests it was also proved that cold storage is both advisable and practical.

8. Bog engineering. This study included tests of wind machines for protection from frosts, which proved unsatisfactory, and efficiency tests of different types of bog pumps.

9. Cultivated blueberries. The practical demonstration at the Station proved so successful that most commercial plantings of blueberries of the state have been in cranberry counties.

There have been many additions and improvements at the Cranberry Station, the latest being a new laboratory and library building operated by scientists and assistants. Professors and a personnel of about twenty-two staff the old and new buildings.

Important meetings of growers and cranberry clubs are held at the new library, and lectures and information given on every pertinent subject by Dr. Chester E. Cross, Dr. R. M. Devlin, Dr. Karl H. Deubert, Professor W. E. Tomlinson, and Extension Specialist Professor I. E. Demoranville.

The information obtained at the Cranberry Station has become so valuable that the Station has become a center for growers seeking information and advice. Special charts covering pest and weed control are prepared and sent out each year. Growers are urged to keep abreast of new trends and developments and to bring their problems to the Station so that they may upgrade their operations and keep Massachusetts the number one cranberry-growing state.

More than 200 members of the Cape Cod Cranberry Growers' Association attended the annual meeting in August, 1975. Byron S. Peterson, agricultural statistician for the United States Department of Commerce, announced that the cranberry harvest for the current year was forecast as 2,256,000 barrels in the United States as a whole, the Massachusetts harvest accounting for 950,000 barrels.

Dr. Chester E. Cross, director of the Cranberry Experiment Station, stated that the cranberry industry would have produced a two-million barrel crop for the sixth consecutive year.

John C. Decas, representing Decas Brothers, an independent firm, said that they expected to handle more fresh berries in 1975 than in previous years. Their firm normally handles between fifty and eighty thousand barrels of which 60 per cent is fresh fruit. The balance is sold to foreign markets and canners and processors in the New Jersey area.

The federal government and Ocean Spray have each allocated $100,000.00 to educate Europeans to eat and cook cranberry products. This report was made by Robert S. FitzSimmonds, director of international marketing for the Agriculture Department. Since taste preferences differ in Europe from those in the United States, a concentrated effort will be made to modify those tastes and to increase sales abroad.

The Cape Cod Cranberry Growers' Association presently has 245 members of which at least 200 are active growers. Its elected officers for 1975-76 are: President, Kenneth D. Beaton; First Vice-President, David B. Mann; Second Vice-President, John C. Decas; Secretary-Treasurer, Irving E. Demoranville. Directors include George J. Andruck, William A. Atwood, Clark Griffith, Arthur M. Handy, Robert B. Hiller, Paul E. Morse, Alfred L. Pappi, Robert H. St. Jacques and Willard A. Rhodes.

Processing Cranberries

he Indians were the first processors of cranberries in this country. They stored fresh and dried berries as part of their winter food supply. Dried cranberries, added to deer fat and dried meat, made a nourishing and easily stored product called "pemmican".

They also preserved the berries in crocks filled with cold fresh water, a method followed extensively throughout cranberry areas up until fairly recent times. Samples of these raw-packed cranberries were sufficiently preserved to be palatable even after several years, they discovered.

The fresh water method was used in supplies on sailing vessels as part of the regular diet of the sailors, even when the voyage encompassed three or four years. The high acidity and small amount of sugar, together with the benzoic acid naturally present in cranberries seemed to retard spoilage and act as a preservative.

The first recorded account of storing fresh cranberries was in a letter dated January 19, 1828 when William Underwood, a supplier in Boston, wrote to Captain Stanwood of the Augusta:

"Dear Sir:

Enclosed you have invoice of pickles, sauces, mustards and preserves of first quality. I have invoiced them considerably less than first quality goods can be purchased in London, which will be some guide to you. Should you not be able to sell them for more than cost and charges in South America, it will, I think, be best to take them to Manila. The cranberries in the bottles are preserved without sugar. I name this because should any person purchase them for sweetmeats they would be disappointed. They are to be used precisely as if purchased fresh from the market, and will keep any length of time before the cork is drawn. Any English people will understand them, and should you fall in with any Men-of-War they will be very agreeable for ship stores, for cabin use, and for any American families who wish for cranberry sauce. The cranberry jam is a sweetmeat and usually brings a high price; I have frequently sold it in India for $1.50 per jar. You will use your own judgment and invest the proceeds as you think best, but I should prefer to have some Manila hemp or sugar."

"Your honorable servant,
William Underwood"

(taken from Bulletin 481 — Agricultural Experiment Station — University of Massachusetts.)

It is interesting to note that Abiel Simpsom, of Providence, Rhode Island, took out one of the early patents on food preservation, issued December 2, 1862. His description claimed: "The merchantable package of cranberries preserved in their natural condition by being submerged in water, as a new manufacture or article of trade." His invention consisted of packing cranberries in water in hermetically sealed packages or jars.

Housewives have canned cranberries with sugar by heating and sealing in glass containers ever since sugar became an easily acquired product.

The first commercial venture and the first cranberry-preserving factory was started in Wareham, Massachusetts in 1898. Operating on a small scale, Mr. R. C. Randall made jam and a cranberry syrup called "Ruby Phosphate", sealing his products in glass jars. Although his products sold readily and at an apparent profit, the operation was discontinued in 1901.

Several small kitchen-type factories were in operation in Boston and Providence, but it was not until 1912, when the United Cape Cod Cranberry Company was formed, that the canned cranberry industry became established and the business began to grow.

Marcus L. Urann, president of the United Cape Cod Cranberry Company, was the first to visualize the possibilities in manufactured cranberry products. From a small factory in South Hanson, Massachusetts, which packed about 5000 cases of cranberry sauce a year, has developed a great industry, packing more than 4,000,000 cases annually.

While practicing law in Boston, Mr. Urann was also developing cranberry bogs in Plymouth County. The bogs were owned by United Cape Cod Cranberry Company, Mr. Urann, President; the other offices held by Massachusetts business men.

Disturbed by the quantities of berries rotting behind screen houses for want of a market for fresh fruit, Mr. Urann's remedy for the situation was processing. Insisting that the cranberry sauce sold by the company must be like "home-made" he developed the recipe, helped stir the first batch, designed the labels, canned it and went out on the road and sold it. His energy and perserverance, and the progress made in utilizing the fruit profitably, gave Mr. Urann the nickname of "Cranberry King".

Ten years later he hired Ocean Spray's first food broker, the Arthur G. Curren Company of Boston. Others followed, and in 1954, twenty-six brokers were honored for twenty-five or more years of service with Ocean Spray.

After World War I other companies began processing, the two most outstanding being A. D. Makepeace Company of Wareham, Massachusetts, and Cranberry Products Company of New Egypt, New Jersey. Because all three of these companies were interested in production of quality products and growth of the industry, they decided, in 1930, to merge in a cranberry growers' cooperative.

First called Cranberry Canners, Inc., the cooperative kept the brand name "Ocean Spray" and the four canning plants owned by the merging companies became the property of the Massachusetts and New Jersey growers who formed the cooperative.

The first Board of Directors meeting was held on August 25, 1930. Elected by the twelve-member board were: President and General Manager, Marcus L. Urann; Secretary-Treasurer, John Makepeace. Serving on the Board and Manager of Processing Operations in New Jersey was Enoch F. Bills, nephew of Miss Elizabeth Lee, former owner of the New Jersey company. Mr. Bills served in this capacity until his retirement in 1964.

In 1940 twenty-five eastern grower-members of the cooperative visited Wisconsin growers. The result of this visit was the unanimous vote of the Wisconsin Sales Company to join the cranberry cooperative. The next year Oregon and Washington growers followed. At this point the cooperative included 735 growers in all of the cranberry growing areas.

Known as Cranberry Canners, Inc. in 1930, and National Cranberry Association in 1946, its products are handled and marketed under the brand name "Ocean Spray" by the cranberry cooperative renamed, in 1959, Ocean Spray Cranberries, Inc.

Mr. Urann retired as President and General Manager in 1955, and Mr. Makepeace as Secretary-Treasurer in 1957. In the 30th Anniversary address at the Annual Meeting of the Stockholders in 1960, Counsel John R. Quarles said this of his friend and associate of over thirty years: "Marcus was one of the greatest promotors and empire builders I have yet known — He had a vivid, creative imagination. He had unlimited energy and patience and all of it was devoted, seven days a week, fifty-two weeks a year, to promoting the cranberry cooperative movement. To him it was almost a religion, and within limits the end justified the means."

And of Mr. Makepeace: "He was quiet and reserved, rarely speaking in meetings or conferences unless he was called upon or felt strongly on an issue under consideration, but when he spoke, it was always worthwhile to listen — Sometimes he suppressed his irritation until it built up to explosive pressure. He was direct to the point of being ingenuous."

Ocean Spray has weathered storms, as have all businesses; a series of short term managements in the search for leadership to insure the continuity of direction and policy of the cooperative in 1959, a restriction by the U.S. Department of Health, Education and Welfare on the sale of cranberries.

When the producers of Amino Triazole, a weed control compound, applied to the Department for a tolerance, none was given. Since a few growers had experimented with the compound, approved by the Department of Agriculture, the entire cranberry crop was made suspect. Subsequent stories spread through the news media added to the problem and holiday sales fell off drastically. Money normally used for promotion was diverted to testing cranberry products on the market and in warehouses to assure their freedom from the compound. The use of Amino, for any purpose, was banned by Ocean Spray.

In March, 1960, the government granted cranberry growers a subsidy for their 1959 berries which were free of the Amino residue but not sold because of the depressed market. This financial help gave the growers some relief, and in late 1960, sales had started to make a comeback. Instrumental in obtaining the subsidy was Ocean Spray President George C. P. Olsson, working with the officers of the Cranberry Institute.

In May, 1963 Mr. Edward Gelsthorpe was appointed Executive Vice-President and General Manager. He set new goals for the co-operative: new products, improved existing products, modernized production, an aggressive marketing program, and strong emphasis on research and development and quality control. By 1965, Mr. Gelsthrope's program was already making progress and sales were the highest in Ocean Spray's history.

Mr. Gelsthorpe resigned in June 1968 and was succeeded by Mr. Edwin F. Lewis, formerly Director of Marketing. During this period sales and returns continued to increase. The 1971 crop was the largest in history, Ocean Spray receiving the largest amount of cranberries ever delivered to them. In January 1970, Mr. Lewis was elected President and Chief Executive Officer.

Mr. Harold Thorkilsen succeeded Mr. Lewis in 1972 as President and Mr. Olsson became Chairman of the Board of Directors. Sales and returns to members have continued to increase with each new year hitting a new high. With increased sales, slightly smaller crops, and the introduction of the Cranberry Marketing Order which prevented increases in cranberry acreage, crop carry-overs were brought within a manageable level.

Much in the way of plant expansion has taken place since 1970. The largest plant ever undertaken by Ocean Spray was completed in 1970 in Kenosha, Wisconsin. A 67,000 square foot modern metal building for increased warehouse capacity was completed in Bordentown, New Jersey, in 1971. This year a major expansion was completed at the Middleborough plant which consolidated all of the Massachusetts facilities.

Massachusetts can be proud of the fact that Ocean Spray Cranberries, Inc., a cooperative originated in this state, is now the country's major organization for processing and marketing cranberries and cranberry products, and that Massachusetts grower-members account for 45% of the crop.

Present-day Cranberries

The present day cultivated cranberry is larger, juicier and more prolific than its wild-growing ancestor. It has a high acid, low sugar content, is rich in iodine, iron, calcium, potassium and other minerals, in Vitamin C and Vitamin A (the anti-infection vitamin), and has other nutritional values.

The states where cranberries are cultivated extensively are Massachusetts, New Jersey, Oregon, Washington, and Wisconsin. They are not grown commercially south of New Jersey for two prime reasons; they do not adapt favorably in warmer areas, and fungus diseases are more prevalent in a warmer climate. Of the states producing the most cranberries commercially, Massachusetts ranks first in cranberry acreage and production, producing about 45% of the total United States output.

There are fifty-odd varieties of cranberries grown, averaging in size about one-half inch in diameter, and varying in form from round to pear shape. It has been discovered that the varieties with fine vines, short upright branches and low seed count are generally more productive and disease-resistant.

The better known varieties are Early Black, Howes, Bugle, Centennial, Holliston, Matthews, McFarlin, and Smalley Howes. They are all fancy berries and preferred for table use. Of interest to Cape Codders is the information that two of the three oldest cultivated varieties, the Howes and the Smalley Howes, originated in Bassett Swamp, East Dennis, and the third, Early Blacks, in neighboring Harwich.

The two kinds grown in the majority of the bogs in Barnstable County (Cape Cod) and Plymouth County (93% of the whole acreage, and therefore most favored) are the Early Blacks and the Howes.

Early Blacks ripen to a deep red color in early September (in some years late August), are a good producer, easily picked with scoops or by machine, keep well and make excellent sauce. Its dark red color makes it valued for juice and canning.

The Howes, grown in about equal proportion to the Early Black, is lighter red in color but matures later. It has a high pectin content which makes it desirable for canning, sauce and jelly.

Both of these varieties are firm, keep well, and are used extensively for packing and marketing fresh. They are grown more extensively the country over than all other varieties put together. They have stood the test of wide cultivation and are still superior in color, flavor and total appreciation.

Eli Howes and Captain Cyrus Cahoon, together with Abel D. Makepeace, under whose guidance cranberry growing became an important industry, are credited with securing the wide acceptance of these leading varieties. They were the great agricultural leaders who brought so much wealth to southeastern Massachusetts, a wealth we continue to enjoy today.

Present day harvesting is not the social occasion that it was in the early years of neighborhood cranberry growing. With increased demand and production, and the introduction of mechanical pickers, it has become industrialized and non-personalized.

The development and use of mechanical pickers began shortly after World War II, and today more than 90% of the country's cranberries are harvested in this manner. In Massachusetts the Darlington picker is most commonly used. Similar to a self-powered lawnmower in appearance, it is guided over the vines by a worker. Its rotating teeth comb the berries from the vines with the forward motion of the machine. The berries drop on a conveyor belt which carries them to a box on a guide bar. Full boxes are placed on trucks and carried to receiving stations and processing plants.

Another method used is the wet pick. The bog is flooded to a depth of about a foot of fresh water. Mechanical water reels, like huge egg beaters, create turbulence in the water, dislodging the ripe berries which float to the top, giving the appearance of a bright red counterpane. Wooden booms gently push the berries to the shore where they are moved by conveyor belts into waiting trucks.

Did you ever wonder why there are so few "bad" cranberries among the fresh berries that you buy at your neighborhood grocery store or supermarket?

Ocean Spray describes the sorting and screening process for us: "After the cranberries are delivered to an Ocean Spray plant, they are cleaned of any chaff (leaves, sticks, vines or grass) by passing through a machine which blows out the chaff. And then *THE BERRY HAS TO BOUNCE SEVEN TIMES* over wooden barriers four inches high. If it doesn't bounce, it's discarded. Firm berries then go to the screening room where a conveyor belt carries them between rows of inspectors who further discard those not up to Ocean Spray standards of appearance. From there the berry that the Cape Cod Indians called "sassamanesh" is either sold fresh or converted into juice or other products, and thus finds its way into hundreds of diversified recipes which those Indians and early settlers could not have imagined.

Conclusion

In the early 17th century a brave and dedicated group of people, hardly more than a handful, made a perilous journey to a wild and strange new world. In the face of isolation, privation and hardship, they forged a proud and independent nation with complete faith in their ability to be self-sustaining, to uphold their rights, and to be self-governing.

While iron alone did not create a new nation, the stability that it brought by being self supporting, and the release from dependence on supplies from a monarchy 3000 miles away and its resulting taxes, gave encouragement and support to the Colonists' decision to be independent.

Although the manufacture of iron has traveled westward with resultant prosperity and fame, its successor in the Cape Cod swamplands, the thriving cranberry industry, flourishes and will continue to do so as long as Americans gather around the Thanksgiving table.

Cannonballs and cranberries — symbols of American talent, ingenuity, imagination and muscle.

The End.

Bibliography

1. Blast Furnaces of Carver — W. B. Murdock
2. Bourne 1622 — 1937 — Keene
3. Earning A Living On Olde Cape Cod — Marion Vuilleumier
4. Economics and Social History of New England 1620 — 1789 — William Weeden
5. Glimpses of Early Wareham — Daisy Washburn Ryder
6. History of Barnstable County — Devo
7. History of Early Settlement of Bridgewater, Massachusetts — Nahum Mitchell
8. History of Plymouth County — Reverend N. W. Everett
9. History of Town of Middleboro, Massachusetts — Thomas Weston
10. Pioneer Iron Works — Mary Stetson Clarke
11. Plympton Town Records 1703 — 1781
12. Settlement and Growth of Duxbury — Dorothy Wentworth
13. Ship Building On North River — Briggs
14. The Bradford History of "Plimouth Plantation"
15. The Cranberry Industry In Massachusetts — Byron S. Peterson, Chester E. Cross, Nathaniel Tilden
16. The Cranberry and Its Culture — Benjamin Eastwood
17. The Early Planters of Scituate — Pratt
18. The Fruits and Fruit Trees of America — A. J. Downing
19. The Pilgrim Republic — John A. Goodwin
20. The Small Fruit Culturist — Andrew S. Fuller
21. The Story of the "Old Colony" of New Plymouth — Samuel Eliot Morrison
22. The Story of Duxbury, Massachusetts — 1637 — 1937 — E. Waldo Lang
23. These Fragile Outposts — Barbara Chamberlain
24. Tremont Cut Nails — Centennial Catalogue 1819 — 1919 — Tremont Nail Company

Appreciation

I wish to express my sincere appreciation to the following for their interest and cooperation in sharing notes, information, references and sources for study and research. Mrs. Ellis D. Atwood, Kenneth Beaton, Edward Bartholomew, George Bartholomew, Charles H. Bricknell, Dr. Chester E. Cross, John Decas, Mrs. Roberta B. Gray, James S. Kenyon, Jr., Edward Lahr, Arnold Lane, Russell Makepeace, O. Herbert McKinney, Mrs. Carolyn Owen, Robert Rich, Raymond Ryder, Henry Shaw, William S. Sullwold, and to the many Town and County Clerks and Librarians.

A special thanks to Professor Irving E. Demoranville who assisted in locating the sites of old iron bogs and present-day cranberry bogs.

CRANBERRY BREAD

2	cups all-purpose sifted flour	¾	cup orange juice
1	cup sugar	1	T. grated orange rind
1½	teaspoons double acting baking powder	3	T. liquid shortening (salad oil)
½	teaspoon soda	½	cup chopped nuts
1	teaspoon salt	2	cups Fresh or Frozen Cranberries coarsely chopped
1	egg, well beaten		

Sift together flour, sugar, baking powder, soda and salt. Combine well beaten egg, orange juice, orange rind and cooking oil. Make a well in dry ingredients and add egg mixture all at once. Mix only to dampen. Carefully fold in nuts and cranberries. Spoon into greased loaf pan (9x5x3"). Spread corners and sides slightly higher than center. Bake in moderate oven (350° F.) for about 1 hour or until crust is brown and toothpick inserted comes out clean. Remove from pan. Cool. Store overnight for easy slicing.

CRANBERRY CRUNCH

1 cup uncooked rolled oats
½ cup flour
1 cup brown sugar
1/3 cup butter or margarine
1 pound can Cranberry Sauce (Jellied or Whole Berry)

Mix oats, flour and brown sugar. Cut in butter or margarine until crumbly. Place half of this mixture in an 8x8" greased baking dish. Cover with cranberry sauce. Top with balance of mixture. Bake 45 minutes at 350° F. Serve hot in squares topped with scoops of vanilla ice cream. Serves 6 to 8.

CRANBERRY PRODUCTS
(Available in United States)

Jellied Cranberry Sauce:
Generic Term .... jellied cranberry sauce
Uses .... as a meat and poultry accompaniment, garnish for cakes and pies, cubed and served with salads and desserts.

Whole Berry Cranberry Sauce:
Generic Term .... whole berry cranberry sauce
Uses .... as a meat and poultry accompaniment, in desserts, salads and sauces.

Low Calorie Jellied Cranberry Sauce:
Generic Term .... low calorie jellied cranberry sauce
Uses .... use as a calorie saving meat and poultry accompaniment, in desserts, salads and sauces.

Deluxe Cranberry-Raspberry Jelly Sauce:
Generic Term .... jellied cranberry-raspberry sauce
Uses .... as a meat accompaniment, in molded salads and desserts, as garnish, as a spread for bread or toast.

Cranberry-Orange Relish:
Generic Term .... cranberry-orange relish
Uses .... a wonderful garnish for meats . . . also excellent as an ingredient in cookies, breads, cakes, salads, desserts . . . a filling for pancakes, tarts, pies . . . a spread for sandwiches, pancakes.

Cranberry Juice Cocktail:
Generic Term .... cranberry juice cocktail
Uses .... for a real thirst quencher, drink plain over ice or chilled . . . excellent as a mixer with other juices, soft drinks and alcoholic beverages . . . can be substituted for wine in many recipes.